Mari Magno, Dipsychus, and Other Poems

Arthur Hugh Clough (1819–61) was the son of a Liverpool merchant who emigrated to South Carolina in 1823. Sent back to England in 1828, he was schooled at Rugby under Dr Thomas Arnold and became a lifelong friend of his family. He was a scholar of Balliol, and became a fellow of Oriel. After persistent religious difficulties he resigned his fellowship in 1848, shortly afterwards publishing a long poem about a Scottish reading party entitled *The Bothie of Tober-na-Vuolich*. The only other long poem published in his lifetime was *Amours de Voyage*, based on his experience of Mazzini's short-lived Roman Republic of 1849. He assisted Florence Nightingale in her Crimean work, having married her cousin Blanche Smith in 1854. At his death he left a substantial *Nachlass* of unpublished poetical material, from which the poems contained in this volume are drawn.

Anthony Kenny was born in Liverpool in 1931, and was educated at Upholland College and the Pontifical Gregorian University in Rome. From 1963 to 1989 he was at Balliol, first as Fellow and Tutor in Philosophy, and then as Master of the College. Subsequently he became Warden of Rhodes House, President of the British Academy, and Chair of the Board of the British Library. He is the author of some forty books, including *Arthur Hugh Clough: A Poet's Life* (Continuum, 2005).

D0813447

Fyfield*Books* aim to make available some of the great classics of British and European literature in clear, affordable formats, and to restore often neglected writers to their place in literary tradition.

Fyfield*Books* take their name from the Fyfield elm in Matthew Arnold's 'Scholar Gypsy' and 'Thyrsis'. The tree stood not far from the village where the series was originally devised in 1971.

Roam on! The light we sought is shining still.
Dost thou ask proof? Our tree yet crowns the hill,
Our Scholar travels yet the loved hill-side

from 'Thyrsis'

ARTHUR HUGH CLOUGH

Mari Magno, Dipsychus, and Other Poems

Edited with an introduction by
ANTHONY KENNY

Fyfield*Books*

CARCANET

First published in Great Britain in 2014 by
Carcanet Press Limited
Alliance House
Cross Street
Manchester M2 7AQ

www.carcanet.co.uk

FSC
www.fsc.org
MIX
Paper from
responsible sources
FSC® C014540

A CIP catalogue record for this book is available
from the British Library

ISBN 978 1 84777 255 8

The publisher acknowledges financial assistance from Arts Council England

Supported by
ARTS COUNCIL
ENGLAND

Typeset by XL Publishing Services, Exmouth
Printed and bound in England by SRP Ltd, Exeter

CONTENTS

INTRODUCTION

1. Arthur Hugh Clough

In the latter part of the nineteenth century it was not uncommon to canonise, as the great poets of the Victorian age, a quartet whose members were Tennyson, Browning, Matthew Arnold and Arthur Hugh Clough. The reputation of the first three endured, but at the end of the century Clough was expelled from the pantheon. In the first half of the twentieth century Lytton Strachey sniggered at Clough's association with Florence Nightingale, and F.R. Leavis exalted the talents of Gerard Manley Hopkins above all four of the original Victorian quartet.

In 1941 Winston Churchill, anxious to secure American co-operation in the fight with Hitler, broadcast some lines from 'Say not the struggle naught availeth' which ended 'Westward, look, the land is bright'. This brought some at least of Clough's poetry back to the national consciousness, and in the post-war years several critics were willing to hail him as the most modern of Victorian poets. The 1960s and 1970s saw a series of biographies and literary studies appear on both sides of the Atlantic. Changing fashions in English departments in universities have led, since 1980, to comparative neglect of Clough's *oeuvre*, though popular editions of the principal poems have continued to appear regularly.

Arthur Hugh Clough was born in Liverpool on 1 January 1819, the son of a cotton merchant of Welsh extraction, and of the daughter of a Yorkshire banker. In the winter of 1822–23 the Cloughs, with their four children, emigrated to Charleston, South Carolina. The family continued to reside in America until 1836, but Arthur was taken back to England in 1828 and a year later entered Rugby school, where he formed a great admiration for the headmaster, Thomas Arnold. He was welcomed into the Arnold family circle where he began lifelong friendships with the headmaster's two eldest sons, Matthew and Thomas.

In 1837 Clough went as a scholar to Balliol College, Oxford. His time at the college was one of religious and emotional crisis. He had been brought up in an evangelical tradition by his mother, and had imbibed liberal Christianity at Rugby, but now he fell for a time under the spell of John Henry Newman and the devotional and ascetic ideals of the Oxford Movement. His diaries and verses of this period show the great strain caused by enduring the pull of conflicting theological traditions. His academic work suffered; he postponed his final examinations, and when he sat them in 1841 he obtained only a second class. He walked to Rugby to tell Arnold that he had failed.

Clough competed unsuccessfully for a Balliol fellowship, but in the following year was elected to a fellowship at Oriel. Shortly afterwards he lost his father, his younger brother, and his second father Thomas Arnold. He was consoled somewhat by the presence in Oxford of the young Arnold brothers, with whom he enjoyed the Oxfordshire excursions later described so engagingly in Matthew's *Scholar Gipsy*.

At Oriel, Clough found himself a colleague of Newman, but by this time he had ceased to feel any attraction to the Tractarian movement. Partly under the influence of Carlyle and German biblical scholarship, he had moved in the opposite direction, and now found Anglican orthodoxy burdensome. It was with reluctance that he subscribed to the Church's Thirty-Nine Articles in 1844, and he began to seek alternatives to his Oriel tutorship, even though Matthew Arnold had joined him as a fellow in the spring of 1845. During his years as a tutor he was a conscientious teacher, and in the summer vacations he took reading parties of his pupils to Braemar and Loch Ness in Scotland. At the beginning of 1848, while his fellowship still had eighteen months to run, he resigned his tutorship, telling the head of his college that he could no longer adhere to the Church's articles.

1848 was a year of revolution throughout Europe, and Clough

spent the spring in Paris, witnessing the French revolution at first hand. He spent the summer writing a narrative poem seventeen hundred verses long, entitled *The Bothie*. The poem was published in November, a month after the final resignation of his Oriel fellowship.

The poem is set in the context of a Scottish reading party, in which the tutor and his pupils bear a strong resemblance to Clough and his young friends. The student hero is a radical poet, Philip Hewson, who combines a belief in the dignity of labour with a keen susceptibility to feminine beauty. After two abortive flirtations, he falls in love with a crofter's daughter, Elspie, and emigrates with her to New Zealand, whither, in reality, young Tom Arnold had emigrated in the previous December.

The Bothie was well received by most reviewers; it sold well and quickly established its author's reputation as a poet. Hard on its heels followed a second publication: in January there appeared *Ambarvalia*, a collection of verse by Clough and his Cambridge friend Thomas Burbidge. Most of its contents are short poems, recalling the trials of student years and the journeys of the religious doubter. 'Qui Laborat, Orat', admired by Tennyson, expresses the tension of prayer to a God who is ineffable; 'The New Sinai' dramatises the conflict between religion and science. There are poems of love and friendship in various moods and metres, and there is a surprisingly frank celebration of fleeting sexual impulse in '*Natura Naturans*'.

From April to August 1849 Clough was in Rome where, since the expulsion of Pius IX in 1848, Mazzini had presided over a short-lived Roman Republic. Clough's letters give a vivid account of Garibaldi's defence of the city against the besieging French army under General Oudinot. With astonishing speed he exploited this experience in poetical form, writing an epistolary novel in five cantos, *Amours de Voyage*. This poem, which is the most enduringly popular of his works, tells the story of Claude, a supercilious Oxford graduate who is initially contemptuous of Rome and of a young English woman he meets on the grand tour, Mary Trevellyn. By the end of the story Claude has fallen in love both with Mary and with the Roman Republic, only to lose them both, as the Trevellyns travel North without him and the French restore the rule of the Pope. The first draft was finished shortly after Clough's return to England, but the final version was not published until 1858 when it appeared in an American journal, *The Atlantic Monthly*.

In the summer of 1849 Clough visited Naples. While there he wrote the most successful of his poems on religious topics, 'Easter Day'. It is an unblinking denial of the Resurrection of Jesus, the central Christian doctrine, in words taken from the Christian scriptures themselves; it accompanies the denial with an unflinching vision of the hopes that are given up by one who abandons Christianity. Believers and unbelievers alike have admired its emotional and intellectual power.

In October of the same year Clough became the head of University Hall, London, a non-sectarian collegiate institution for students attending lectures at University College. He was not happy with his duties there, and he was disappointed in love. He spent the summer in Venice, in which he commenced work on the dramatic poem, *Dipsychus*. During this period he also wrote a sequence of seven sonnets.

At the end of 1851 Clough left University Hall. It was important for him to find alternative employment, because he was now in love with Blanche Smith of Combe Hall, Surrey, to whom he became engaged in 1852. In October 1952 he sailed with W.M. Thackeray to America, where he was warmly welcomed by Emerson, Longfellow, Charles Eliot Norton and other members of Boston literary society. During his travels he wrote a number of poems, which were later collected by his wife under the title 'Songs in Absence'. He had no success, however, in finding a permanent job, and returned to England where his friends had found him a post as examiner in the Education Office, which enabled him to marry Blanche in June 1854.

What time Clough had to spare from his exertions in the Education Office was spent in assisting his wife's cousin Florence Nightingale in her campaign to reform military hospitals. It was he who had escorted her to Calais in 1854 on her first voyage to the Crimean theatre of war. By 1861 his health had broken down, and he was given sick-leave for a foreign tour. He went to Greece and Constantinople, and began to write his last long poetical venture, a series of tales which was to become *Mari Magno*. After a few weeks at home in June 1861 Clough went abroad again, and spent some time in the Pyrenees with the Tennysons. The attempt to recover his health was vain, and he died in November in Florence, where he is buried in the Protestant cemetery.

2. The drama of *Dipsychus*

The verse drama *Dipsychus* was conceived at a very low moment in Clough's life. During the summer vacation of his first unhappy year as Principal of University Hall he was due to visit Switzerland with Matthew Arnold, but he was let down as Matthew raced across Germany in pursuit of a woman. Instead he went alone to Venice. The dramatic date of *Dipsychus* is the feast of the Assumption, 15 August 1850. That was the exact date of the marriage of Matthew's sister Jane to William Edward Foster. Jane had been the object of Arthur's first disappointed love, and he had not yet met the woman who was to become his wife. The year was one when, as he told Thomas Arnold, 'I could have gone cracked at times... with one thing and another'.

Clough revised his early Venetian drafts several times after his return to England, but never brought *Dipsychus* into a form that satisfied him. The poem was left in several incomplete manuscript versions on his death. It presented a difficult editorial problem for his widow, who undertook the posthumous publication of his unpublished poems. The problems presented by the manuscripts were made more severe for Blanche Clough by her distaste for parts of the poem that she regarded as licentious or irreligious. In her first posthumous edition of the poems in 1862 she printed several sections of the work as separate poems. The drama was first presented as a unit – in a highly censored version – in a private edition of 1865. It was offered to the general public in the same form in 1869.

In recent times fuller versions have been published in editions of Clough's works, reproducing more of the material to be found in the manuscripts – notably the Oxford editions of 1951 (H.F. Lowry and others) and of 1974 (F.L. Mulhauser) and the Longman edition of 1995 (J.P. Phelan). It would be wrong to think that these later editions give the full text of a poem previously available in mutilated form. Given Clough's changes of mind, and ultimate indecision, there is no such thing as *the* text of the poem. The situation is similar to that of some of Verdi's operas, such as *Don Carlos*, where several differently structured scores can make an equal claim to authenticity.

In all versions the poem is a Faustian dialogue, set in Venice, between a young ingénu of tender conscience, who is trying to decide on a way of life for himself, and a mysterious but worldly wise interlocutor, who urges him to embark on a conventional career. In the earlier versions of the text the two characters are named Faustulus and Mephisto; in later revisions these names were altered to Dipsychus and the Spirit, and Clough began to use the title *Dipsychus* for the whole poem. The Greek word *dipsychos* is used in the Epistle of St James, for instance in I.8, a verse translated in the Authorised Version as 'A double minded man is unstable in all his ways'.

The character Dipsychus in the dialogue is in some sense identified with the poet himself: he frequently quotes Clough's previous poems as his own compositions. Is the Spirit character to be identified with the Devil, as the name Mephisto suggests – or are we to regard him as the other half of the two-souled man? Either identification would be rash. Dipsychus himself stresses the ambiguous nature of his interlocutor. Early in the dialogue he asks

> What is this persecuting voice that haunts me?
> What? Whence? of whom? How am I to detect?
> Myself or not myself? My own bad thoughts,
> Or some external agency at work
> To lead me who knows whither?

And in a prose epilogue that Clough considered adding to the poem, the poet explains to his uncle:

> Perhaps he wasn't a devil after all. That's the beauty of the poem; nobody can say. You see, dear sir, the thing which is attempted to represent is the conflict between the tender conscience and the world. Now, the over-tender conscience will, of course, exaggerate the wickedness of the world; and the Spirit in my poem may be merely the hypothesis or subjective imagination.

Like Dipsychus, the reader must remain throughout uncertain whether the Spirit is a force for good or evil, and must try to evaluate each of his suggestions on its merits. But whether the Spirit be a true devil or not, he certainly represents the flesh and the world, and at a moment of submission Dipsychus yields to all three: 'the greedy flesh, the world, the Devil – welcome, welcome, welcome'.

Even in a self-portrait it is important to keep clear the distinction between portrayer and portrayed. The author of *Dipsychus*, though he is writing about himself, cannot, as author, be identified with either of the voices he creates. No doubt at various times and in various moods Clough would identify himself now with the ethereal idealism of Dipsychus, now with the jaunty worldliness of Mephisto. But in the poem as presented the criticism that each, by juxtaposition, makes of the other is as much an utterance of the authorial voice as either of the positions criticised.

I shall now summarise the progress of the drama through the succession of scenes as presented in the present edition. I should make clear that the structure of the poem is a matter of controversy. The sequence of some of the most important scenes is left uncertain by the manuscripts, and these scenes have been printed by successive editors in different orders. The order of the scenes is important for the overall interpretation of the poem: in the next section of the introduction I shall defend the ordering that I have preferred.

Introduction

Act I

Scene 1. In the Piazza San Marco, Dipsychus recalls 'Easter Day', and having surveyed the scene concludes that Christ is not risen in Venice any more than in Naples. The Spirit tries to detach him from his theological pondering, and encourages him to take part in the harmless pleasures of the evening – coffee, ices, and the music of Rossini.

Scene 2. Dipsychus admires the lively scene in the Giardini Pubblici. The Spirit informs him that the crowd is celebrating the feast of the Assumption of the Virgin Mary, and draws his attention to the frank display of feminine beauty that is on offer. Dipsychus is ogled by a passing servant girl, but after some hesitation he declines her invitation.

Scene 3. Walking along the quays back towards his hotel, Dipsychus expresses remorse for having ever entertained the thought of fornication – first on the basis of an idealistic view of women as angels, then on a more realistic assessment of the likely fate that awaits a fallen woman. The Spirit encourages him to visit a prostitute, but he is an honest purveyor of sex and does not wish to paint its delights in too glowing colours. Casual fornication, he explains, is not an apple from the tree of knowledge; whatever virginal curiosity may imagine, it leaves one, for better or worse, much as before. The pair return to the Piazza where, as we learn in the following scene, Dipsychus does visit a prostitute, but pays her off without making use of her services.

Scene 4. Back in the hotel the Spirit suggests more socially respectable forms of flirtation: gallantry in the ballroom, followed by a judicious engagement. Dipsychus rejects the social conventions of courtship as tedious and hollow.

Scene 5. A Croatian soldier of the Austrian army of occupation shouts offensively at Dipsychus. The Spirit urges him to avenge the insult by challenging the soldier to a duel. The pair engage in a long discussion about honour, violence, peace, and war.

Dipsychus, though willing to fight in some good cause, will not draw the sword because of some trifling offence. The Spirit mocks at Christian pacifists.

Scene 6. The two sail to the Lido. On the way Dipsychus sings of a dream, in which bells ring out the news that, for good or ill, there is no God. The poem spells out the consequences of atheism for sexual morality and for war and peace and civil order. The Spirit responds with a lively lyric, 'There is no God, the wicked says', which examines the motives which lead people to believe, or disbelieve, in God's existence. A bathe on the Lido gives no pleasure to the Spirit, but greatly cheers Dipsychus. Whereas Act I began with Dipsychus's quotation 'Christ is not risen' it ends with the Spirit's ironic "Tis Easter Day, and on the Lido / Lo Christ the Lord is risen indeed, O'.

There follows an entr'acte entitled 'In a Gondola'. The scene begins and ends with a lyric of Dipsychus comparing and contrasting the pair's three-hour gondola ride with the whole course of life. It is a succession of verses which could be (and in some cases were) published as independent poems: in context these are songs that the two companions sing to each other as the gondoliers take them in the evening along the Grand Canal and out into the Lagoon. Dipsychus's social conscience makes him worry that they are exploiting the poor gondoliers, and the Spirit mocks him for his unworldly idealism. All the best verses are given to the Spirit, culminating in the Gilbertian patter-song 'How pleasant it is to have money!'

Act II
Scene 1 is entitled 'The Academy'. It begins with a lyric which uses two paintings in an exhibition to make a contrast between the active and the contemplative life. Dipsychus wonders what way of life he should adopt: none of the careers he considers presents any attraction. He indicates that he is willing to negotiate a Faustian bargain with the Spirit (whom he addresses, initially, as

Mephistopheles). The Spirit urges him to give up infidelity, and to enter a profession such as the Church or the Law. He offers to find a suitable lady for Dipsychus to propose to, for marriage is almost a sine qua non for worldly respectability.

Scene 2. Dipsychus retires to meditate on the Spirit's advice, in a soliloquy of 160 lines of blank verse. A legal career disgusts him: lawyers make their money out of the dirt in other people's lives. As for marriage, he had hoped for something better than an arranged match. In any form of action, the hardest thing is the choice of the right moment. He weighs up the contrasting dangers of premature action and of excessive delay, and laments the de-personalised nature of modern life. In the end he accepts that his hope of individual, unselfish, heroic action is a romantic dream: there is no alternative to taking a humble part in the world's work. The Spirit, offstage, applauds this common-sense decision.

Scene 3. Once again in the Piazza San Marco Dipsychus contrasts his moods of contentment and disillusion. The Spirit, fearing that he is about to relapse from his resolve of submission to the world, describes the impotence and futility of Dipsychus's life when left to his own devices. This leisured life of principled indecision must be renounced if anything is to be achieved in the world.

Scene 4. Once more Dipsychus tries to delay decision and prolong his present way of life, but the Spirit refuses to be dismissed. There is no alternative to coming to terms with the world of business. Neither poetry, philosophy, nor tutoring will provide him with a living. It is time for him to grow up and forsake dreams and delusions.

Scene 5. In final bargaining Dipsychus tries in vain to persuade the Spirit to take over less than his whole soul. He welcomes the world, and says farewell to his dreams, but tries to include the Faustian bargain itself as a dream. The Spirit reveals that his name is indeed Mephistopheles. But he has other names too, of which his favourite is *Cosmocrator*, ruler of the world – the world that

Dipsychus has at last made up his mind to enter. However, Dipsychus claims that Scripture promises conquest over the world. The Spirit is content to leave time to test which of the pair of them is the stronger. He is willing to bet that Dipsychus, having agreed to submit to the world, will yield forthwith to the temptations he has hitherto resisted.

In the division into two parts, and in the order of the scenes, I have followed in the main the structure of the poem as presented by Blanche Clough in her 1865 edition. My Act I has six scenes instead of five, because she omitted Scene 3, as well as large sections of other scenes. The order of the other scenes in Act I is the same in my edition as in hers, and is indeed dictated by the MSS except for the placement of Scene 6. The scene that I print as an entr'acte appears in the MSS sometimes as belonging to the first part and sometimes as belonging to the second: in the 1865 edition it is the second scene of the second part. The five scenes of my second act correspond to Scenes 3, 4, 5, 6 and 9 of Blanche Clough's second part. Her Scene 1 I regard as an alternative version of Act I, Scene 1, and I have omitted her short Scenes 7 and 8.

The 1974 Oxford edition of Clough's works does not divide *Dipsychus* into two parts, because of uncertainty in the MSS about where one part was to end and the other to begin. It is clear, however, that Clough intended the poem to be divided, and there are a number of differences between the two parts. In the first part the action is firmly placed in Venice; in the second part the occasional references to Venetian surroundings are as often as not purely ornamental. In the first part there is no real converse between the characters: the Spirit merely adds ironic comments to Dipsychus's soliloquies; in the second part the two engage in colloquy, and indeed in bargaining. In the first part the Spirit's temptations are of a crude, and initially gross, kind: he is Belial rather than Mephistopheles. In the second part, by contrast, he speaks with the voice of Clough's respectable seniors. In the first part, Dipsychus resists the Spirit's suggestions, while in the second he in the end accepts the demand to 'submit'.

In considering the division between the parts, the scene that editors have found most difficult to place on the basis of the MSS evidence is 'In a Gondola'. I have resolved the problem by treating it as an entr'acte. It is indeed structured in quite a different way from the other scenes of the two parts, being a sequence of lyrics which seem to be connected only by free association, quite different from the interrupted monologues of Act I and the colloquies of Act II.

Dipsychus, in Act I, successfully resists three temptations: to carnality, to aggression, and to atheism. The tempter represents successively the flesh, the world, and the devil. But the triptych of temptation also corresponds to the classical triad of the three possible lives, familiar to Clough from his reading and teaching of Plato and Aristotle: the life of pleasure, the life of honour, and the life of thought. In classical psychology these three lives in their turn corresponded to three parts of the soul: the appetitive part, the irascible part, and the rational part. The first temptations allure Dipsychus's appetitive part; the insult scene is the challenge to his irascible part; the philosophico-theological discussions concern his rational part.

While the temptations of Act I are such as beset all mankind, in one form or other, the problems of Act II concern the specific choice of a career for an individual with the gifts, ideals, and history of Clough himself. This part puts the question whether any of the careers on offer can be chosen without a betrayal of those ideals, and whether an idealist can frame his own life rather than fit himself into slots provided by the world. The movement of thought, and the duplication between the two parts of the poem, once again follow an Aristotelian pattern. In a similar manner, Aristotle, having commenced his ethical treatise with a treatment of the traditional choice between three lives, reduces the choice in the final book of the *Nicomachean Ethics* to the choice between the active and the contemplative life.

Dipsychus, in the end, opts for neither life. He explicitly, in the first scene of Act II, renounces the contemplative life of the poet, and in Scene 4 the heroic life of action such as Byron led in his last days. Instead he chooses to 'submit'. To what? To Victorian respectability. This was what Clough himself did, in marrying and taking a job with the civil service, and effectively giving up poetry for several years. But this did not mean that he submitted uncritically to Victorian values. It is surely significant that in *Dipsychus* the case for respectability is placed in the mouth of Mephistopheles.

3. The text and the manuscripts of Dipsychus

The original MSS of *Dipsychus* are in the Bodleian Library in Oxford (Eng Poet d.133-9). They were given titles by Mrs Eleanor Clough, the poet's daughter-in-law, and they fall into three groups:

1. Clough's Venice notebook, which contains drafts of many sections, plus other material (V).
2. 'Longest First Copy' version, in three notebooks, entitled Dipsychus A I/II/III.
3. 'Second and latest copy (incomplete)' entitled Dipsychus B.

There is evidence that these three groups represent successive stages of composition: many lines that appear as emendations in Dipsychus A are written out fair in Dipsychus B, and lines struck out in A fail to appear in B. But the evidence is not unambiguous, and in many cases it is clear that the poet changed his mind more than once.

The relation between the three notebooks of Dipsychus A is a matter of controversy. The Oxford editors labelled Dipsychus A II and III (Scene I.5 to end) *First Revision* and Dipsychus A Scenes I.1–4 *Second Revision*, assigning an order to the two on the basis of the naming of the characters Faustulus and Mephistopheles in II and III, and Dipsychus and the Spirit in I. Two things are misleading about the titles *First* and *Second Revision*. In the first place, given the chaotic nature of the Venice notebooks, with no indication of divisions or order of the poems, and no title given for the whole, Dipsychus A I–III represents the very first redaction of the drama, not a revision. Secondly, it is doubtful whether there is any case for regarding A I as later in time, simply on the basis of the nomenclature. Clough does not seem until a final stage to have made up his mind about the naming of the characters. S and M appear as alternative names in a passage of the Venice notebook, and F and M occur alongside D and S in A III. In fact, the three notebooks are best treated as a single recension, as the Oxford editors in practice did.

However, J.P. Phelan, in his edition of selected poems (Longman, 1995) argued that a considerable time elapsed between the composition of the two halves of A. The second portion, A II–III, he wrote, was almost certainly written before Clough left for the USA in 1852, but A I cannot have been written before late 1854. For the latter part of the last century critics seem to have accepted the Oxford editors' judgement that, apart from some late revisions to the song 'As I sat at the café I said to myself', Clough 'seems to have put the poem aside, unfinished, after 1851'. All this changed when Phelan published an article, 'The textual evolution of Clough's Dipsychus and the Spirit', in which he claimed that six scenes were not written until 1854 at the very earliest.

Phelan offered two principal arguments for this. In the Gondola scene there is a long passage in which the Spirit praises Palladian churches in preference to Gothic buildings, and makes a reference to 'Ruskin's d—d pretence'. Phelan sees this as a reference to the attack on Palladio in Ruskin's *Stones of Venice*, of which the relevant volumes did not appear until late 1853. However, in context, 'Ruskin's d—d pretence' does not concern Palladio, but only the Doge's Palace; and the 'pretence' consists in exaggerated praise. Such praise is easy to find in the *Seven Lamps of Architecture*, published in 1849, and its hyperbolic nature was later admitted by Ruskin himself.

Phelan believed that he had found another allusion that is unambiguous in its reference to late 1854. The Spirit, in Scene 3, defends prostitution as providing women with a way of starting to earn a living. They go on to marry, or superintend, or are sent out by Sidney Herbert to colonise. This passage, Phelan argued, refers to Herbert's tenure of office as Secretary of War at the time of the Crimean War, during which he asked Florence Nightingale to superintend an expedition of nurses to Scutari. Sidney Herbert did become Colonial Secretary in 1855, but it was not at that time that he sent women abroad. Earlier, in 1849, he and his wife founded the Female Emigration Fund to provide assisted female emigration to the colonies so that women could marry and breed a white population there.

In the absence of further evidence we cannot conclude that A was written any later than 1850. One might well argue, however, that B was written after Clough's return from the United States, and perhaps after his marriage. We know that during Arthur's absence in America Blanche came across a MS called Dipsychus. She disliked what she saw, and Arthur was horrified that she had seen it: 'please don't read it yet' he wrote to her. While in the US he wrote a piece called 'Dipsychus continued' (its American origin was established by Katherine Chorley on the basis of the water-marks of the paper on which it was written). In this piece Dipsychus, now an elderly Lord Chief Justice, is confronted by a beggar woman, an ex-prostitute, with whom he had consorted in earlier days before his marriage. 'In old times / You called me Pleasure – my name now is Guilt'.

The piece is a mawkish one, rightly described by Blanche when she was editing it for the 1865 edition as 'most unsatisfactory'. It seems clearly aimed at conciliating those (including Blanche herself) who were repelled by the more licentious parts of the original Dipsychus. For our present purposes the thing to note is that such a palinode, while relevant to MS A, would be quite inappropriate to MS B in which no prostitute appears. It is natural to conclude that while A was complete before Clough left for the US and was the MS that Blanche saw and disliked, manuscript B dates from after his return.

Whatever its precise date, it is a matter of general agreement that B, though incomplete, is the latest of the MSS. It might be thought therefore that it is the version to publish, as representing the latest stage of authorial intention. Blanche Clough's 1865 edition is indeed closer to B than it is to A, and closer to B than any modern edition is. Modern editors have rejected B because of its obvious marks of bowdlerisation. Phelan published A in its entirety; while the Oxford editors used B as the basic text for the scenes it contains, but supplemented it with material from A which they judged had been suppressed on grounds of impropriety. Accordingly, the Oxford editions correspond to no stage of Clough's own development of the poem.

Both A I and B can be seen as alternative supplements to A II and A III. It is not easy to grasp the relationship of the different MSS, and it may be helpful to compare the poem to a pantomime horse. The manuscripts give us one pair of back legs, and two pairs of front legs, one pair being larger than the other. Different editors have differed in their choice of which of the front pairs was the fittest match for the back pair. In the earliest edition Blanche Clough started from the smaller front legs – a new and improved pair, in her view – and trimmed the back legs to bring them into line. The Oxford editors opted for the smaller front legs, but patched them from time to time with material from the larger pair. Phelan opted outright for the larger pair of front legs.

My own edition is, like the Oxford one of 1974, a hybrid one. It differs from it in four ways. First, I have made much fuller use of early material from the Venice notebook when I thought it presented a better text than the later editions. Second, I have also included passages which were cancelled by the poet in MSS A and B when I thought his first thoughts were better than his second. Third, I have omitted two scenes (Scenes VIII and XIII in the Oxford text) that seemed to me to reduplicate material already better presented elsewhere. Finally, I have dispensed with the prose prologue and epilogue with which at one time Clough intended to frame the drama.

I conclude by listing the sources of the texts offered for each scene:

Act I
Scene 1: B, except for lines 24–80, 94–96 and 107–108, which are from A.

Scene 2: Lines 1–66 from B, lines 67–96 from A.
Scene 3: A, except for lines 71–83 and 237–44 which are from V.
Scene 4: Lines 1–12 from V, then all from A.
Scene 5: A, except for lines 201–10 from V.
Scene 6: A, except for lines 22–29 from V.

Entr'acte: Lines 1–69, 75–82, 110–13 from B; 70–74, 89–109, 114–55, 228–307 from A; 83–88 from V; 156–227 from a variety of MSS.

Act II
Scene 1: A, except for lines 28–67 from V.
Scene 2: A, except for lines 93–96 from V.
Scene 3: A throughout.
Scene 4: A except for lines 68–99 from V.
Scene 5: A throughout.

4. The composition of *Mari Magno*

Mari Magno or *Tales on Board* is a suite of poems written during the last year of the poet's life. In the spring of 1861, having taken six months sick-leave from his duties in the Council Office, Clough was advised by his doctors to spend time in a warmer climate. Between April and June he travelled alone on the continent, visiting Athens and Constantinople. After a brief return to England he recrossed the Channel, travelled in France, and spent some time in the Pyrenees with Alfred Tennyson and his family. Joined by his wife in September, he journeyed with her to Florence, where he died on 13 November.

Prior to these final travels, Clough had written no original poetry for eight years. Shortly before he left England he received a letter from R.W. Emerson saying 'Your muse is silent, and too long'. He rose to the challenge by writing a number of verse tales in a style, modelled on Crabbe, that was very different from that of his earlier poems. Initially, he composed the tales as independent stories, but having written the first four poems he conceived the idea of uniting them within a single structure on the model of Chaucer's *Canterbury Tales*. The suite was originally to be entitled 'A Modern Pilgrimage', but later Clough decided that the 'pilgrims' should be fellow passengers on an ocean liner sailing across the Atlantic. They should tell each other a story or two for each night of the voyage, and love and marriage should be the theme common to all the tales.

The first poem, written on the spring continental tour, is entitled '*Primitiae* or Third Cousins'. The hero of the story, at the age of twelve, meets a cousin Emily, two years his senior, who is one of a clutch of daughters of a Welsh clergyman. He and Emily have a number of adventures together. On a later visit they are invited by the hero's senior schoolfellow, Helston, to join him in his yacht; but the pair prefer to row to a private beach where there is kissing. At the age of eighteen the hero visits the family again, in the vicar's retirement rectory, for a ball which he finds boring. The next day, however, he finds he is attracted to Emily and has missed an opportunity. A year later he returns, and shows off his university learning. He appears all head and no heart, and the visit is a failure. Emily, now Emilia, becomes more distant, and the poem ends with the hero, on the grand tour after taking his Oxford degree, meeting her in Switzerland with Helston whom she has recently married. He stays with her at her new home, and describes the college fellowship that he has won. She says that the life of a don would be a waste of his talents, and that if he gives it up he will rise above her and his family. He takes her advice and the poem ends.

Some readers have been put off the poem by its jog-trot tetrameters, but it is a sensitive and convincing portrayal of the difficulties of male adolescence, and the hero's realisation of his love only when it is too late resembles that of Claude in *Amours de Voyage*. During his brief return to England in 1861 Clough himself thought well enough of the poem to give a copy to the historian J.A. Froude as a wedding present.

A second poem which Clough's widow believed to have been written on this continental tour tells the tale of a couple called Edmund (20) and Emma (18). The two join in childish games on a summer night in the northern mountains, and Edmund makes too free with Emma's Christian name. Having been too serious at school, Edmund now enjoys riding, swimming, and hiking, but still retains an ascetic bent. The poem then purports to quote passages from a notebook written beside Wordsworth's wishing-gate. Should impulse be law? Or should one's wishes be winnowed? What is love? Surely it must be all-conquering if it be love at all, and it must include lofty fellowship of mind with mind. Edmund feels that he cannot really be in love with Emma because he is not totally overwhelmed. Whether he really loves her only absence will show, and so he goes away on tour. On his return he finds his father sick and has to drudge to provide for his family. Worn out, he is sent to the seaside for his health, and here meets Emma by chance upon the shore. The two fall into each other's arms and are married within weeks. The poem ends with a stanza to the effect that love is fellow-service.

The poem contains some fine lines, but it is not a success. The notebooks of the hero and heroine are not well integrated into the story; the final reunion and marriage is a hasty and unconvincing episode; and the concluding piece about love as fellow-service is bafflingly ill-attached. The story does, however, have a clear message: marriage should not be based on a romantic idea of love as an overwhelming obsession.

Clough crossed again to France early in July and spent the middle weeks of the month at a watering place near Clermont-Ferrand called Le Mont-Dore, where he had a brief meeting with the Tennysons. In a letter to his wife he described the free and easy relations between the sexes in his hotel. An entertainment by a poetic improviser stimulated his own poetic vein, and he wrote a story, to which he gave the title 'Juxtaposition', about how easy it was in a large hotel to go to the wrong room. In the poem two sisters share a bed; one of them goes downstairs to retrieve her watch, and returns by mistake to a different room. Unknowingly she gets into bed beside a young man. Discovering her mistake in the morning she runs away; but in due course the young man returns the watch, and the pair get married and live happily ever after.

Clough's departure from Mont-Dore on 25 July provided the stimulus for a longer and better inspired poem. Having learnt that the Tennysons were headed for the Pyrenees, he decided to follow them, hoping to join them at Bagnères-de-Luchon. His journey was made mainly by train, but for the first stage, from Mont-Dore to Tulle, he had to use the diligence that carried the mail, the *courier*. He took a seat on this four-horse vehicle, and in due course wrote a vivid account of the journey in two hundred rhymed pentameters, which he entitled 'A la banquette'.

The poem contains some vivid description of the landscape, but the main interest is in the description of the companions on the journey: the *conducteur*, a bibulous baritone; a soldier invalided out of the Italian wars; a peasant abusing an illiterate mayor; a priest with a tale of a sick child healed by the Virgin, and the postillion who caps this with an account of the remarkable cure of his own ailing ass. In characterising his travelling companions Clough seems to have taken as his model the prologue to Chaucer's *Canterbury Tales*, and it was to this poem that he first gave the title 'A Modern Pilgrimage'. It was most likely at this time that he wrote the Edmund and Emma poem that, for reasons unknown to us, Blanche assigned to his earlier continental tour.

Clough reached Bagnères-de-Luchon by the end of July, but he saw little of the Tennysons during August, spending most of his time in solitary wandering in the Pyrenees. In bed with diarrhoea on 13 August he wrote a poem, '*Currente Calamo*', that describes a graceful olive-skinned girl driving a donkey. Justly proud of the poem he sent it in his next letter to his wife. During the same period he wrote a self-standing poem, a rendering of the legend of the hunter Actaeon, who was transmuted into a stag, and savaged by his own hounds, because he peeped at the goddess Diana while she was bathing. This poem, like '*Currente Calamo*', may have been a tribute to some Pyrenean beauty briefly glimpsed.

It was shortly after this that Clough drew up a plan for incorporating into a sequence the major poems so far written on his sick-leave: '*Primitiae*', 'Edmund and Emma', 'Juxtaposition', and 'A la banquette' plus '*Currente Calamo*'. It was at this point that he decided that instead of pilgrims to a shrine, his storytellers would be transatlantic voyagers. The sequence would be called *Mari Magno* or *Tales on Board*, and it would end with the poem 'Where lies the land' as an envoi.

A little later Clough wrote a Preface to the sequence, again on the pattern of Chaucer, describing the passengers on the vessel: a lawyer, a rural dean, a returning American tourist, and the narrator, a youth about whom we are told little. The existing stories are now distributed between the characters and assigned a time: '*Primitiae*' is told by the lawyer on the first night of the voyage, on the second night 'Edmund and Emma' is told by the clergyman and 'Juxtaposition' by the American, while on the third night 'A la banquette' is recited by the narrator as 'My Tale'.

The storytelling is triggered, in a newly composed preface, by a discussion between the lawyer and the clergyman on the nature of marriage. Is marriage bliss, or is it discipline? It is the American who suggests how to resolve the disagreement:

> You'll reason on till night and reason fail;
> My judgement is you each shall tell a tale;
> And as on marriage you can not agree,
> Of love and marriage let the stories be.

The title of the sequence, as so often in Clough, bears a double meaning. *Mari Magno* is a natural title for a series of tales told aboard ship; but it also echoes a famous passage of Lucretius, beginning 'Suave mari magno', which describes the pleasure someone safe on shore can take in watching ships battling with the elements at sea. So possibly the poem is meant to represent, from the point of view of someone yet unmarried, as the narrator is, the various things that can go wrong before or after a wedding.

However, once he had decided on the theme and structure of *Mari Magno* Clough went on to add new stories, to occupy the fourth night of the voyage. The mate of the ship tells how a French governess returning to France from her Anglo-Irish family is stranded on a Liverpool pier after missing her connection to

Bordeaux. The ship's captain takes her in and marries her out of pity. An artillery officer, who has joined the group, questions whether the captain may not be merely adding another to a collection of wives in every port. He goes on to tell his own story from the Crimean war, in which an elderly war tourist marries a woman he has rescued from the unwelcome attentions of a group of French soldiers.

It was not until 31 August that Clough was reunited with the Tennysons, at Luz in the Pyrenean region. While he was with them he wrote the next of the *Mari Magno* stories, for the fifth night. It was assigned to the clergyman as his second tale. In the story, Edward and Jane marry at 21 and have nine years of blissful marriage. Edward, however, falls ill and is sent abroad for his health, while his wife goes to her mother. He finds solitary wandering dismal. He wants to return, but his wife says it is all too soon. At his *table d'hôte* he falls for a beautiful Junoesque woman who entices him into her bedroom. He is full of remorse for this lapse, and resolves that he cannot ever go home to his wife. She will remain with her mother, he will take lodgings by his office, and support her financially each quarter day. Later in London he meets his partner in adultery, now a streetwalker. He is summoned home to the sickbed of a daughter. The daughter recovers, and he resumes normal married life.

Of all the *Mari Magno* series, this poem was the one most admired when first published, and most reviled in the twentieth century. Both reactions are based on a false premise: that we are meant to admire Edward's egotistical penitence. The clerical narrator seems to do so; but the poet surely meant us to accept rather the view expressed by the artillery captain that the husband's leaving his family was no less sinful than his adultery. The poem, we are told, was written in a single night, and when he read it out to the Tennysons Clough was reduced to tears.

On 13 September Clough learnt that his wife, recovered from the birth of her daughter Blanche Athena at the beginning of August, planned to cross the channel to take care of him. He left the Tennysons and travelled to Paris to meet her. The pair travelled southward by slow stages, reaching Florence in October and spending a month there until Arthur died on 13 November.

In these last days Clough continued, frenetically, to compose poetry, keeping a small notebook under his pillow. During the last days of October he got out of bed and began making a fair copy. When he was no longer able to write, he began to dictate to his wife until he broke down, leaving her to complete the poem from the scribbles in his diary. It was the final story in the *Mari Magno* series, the lawyer's second tale, told on the last night of the voyage just before the liner reaches Boston.

In the story, a 25-year-old Oxford college fellow, Philip, staying alone in a Highland inn after a reading party, falls in love with a parlour maid, Christian (who gives her name to the story). He attempts to resist temptation, but finally seduces her. He escorts her by sea to Glasgow, secures an upgrade for her cabin, and teaches her astronomy. At Glasgow he takes lodgings with her family. He plans to marry her, but reveals to her family that in order to do so he would have to forfeit a fellowship worth £300 a year. He goes to Oxford for the college audit, and on his return to Glasgow discovers that the family, distrustful of his intentions and anxious to get the girl out of his clutches, has emigrated to Australia. He follows them across the ocean but cannot trace them. On his return he becomes a successful journalist, serves on government commissions, and marries a Lady Mary. Later, his former lover, now married with a family, turns up in England from Australia. The two women make friends, and Christian hands over her eldest son – Philip's – to the childless Lady Mary.

What does the suite as a whole have to tell us about its professed topic of love and marriage? The tales of the lawyer and clergyman fit a symmetrical pattern: the first stories of each tell of troubles getting in the way of a marriage, the second stories of each concern also strains supervening on marriage. The characters of the two narrators are sharply contrasted: the clergyman is puritanical and sanctimonious, the lawyer romantic and liberal. The officer's and mate's stories illustrate, as does the American's, how a marriage may be the unexpected result of a contingent accident. But we are left uncertain in their case whether the marriage will turn out happy: only 'Juxtaposition' tells us explicitly that the marriage was a happy one.

It is clear how all these stories illustrate different motives for marriage and the different consequences they may have. But it is not clear how 'My Tale' fits into a sequence on love and marriage. True, the *conducteur* sings a song regretting the loss of youthful ardour, but this occupies only a small part of the long account of the coach journey. It has been suggested that the empty banality of the episodes narrated is meant to illustrate the disappointing nature of Clough's own marriage. But there is little evidence that his marriage was at all disappointing, and in any case it is a mistake simply to identify the narrator of *Mari Magno* with the poet himself. The narrator is a young man lacking any serious amatory experience, and the most he has to offer is a series of momentary glimpses of beautiful passers-by – a series into which 'Actaeon' might well have fitted. But though 'My Tale' is not Clough's tale, that does not mean that *Mari Magno* has nothing to tell us about the poet's own experience. Quite the contrary.

5. *Mari Magno* as autobiography

Throughout the tales that make up *Mari Magno* there occur reminiscences of places and events in Clough's life. The frame provided by the westward transatlantic crossing recalls the voyage of the Cunarder sail-and-steam packet *Canada* from Liverpool to Boston in November 1852. The ship carried Thackeray on his way to a lecture tour and Clough seeking his fortune to enable him to marry Blanche Smith. Clough, then 33, was sea-sick for much of the voyage. In the poem the voyage takes place in August, the narrator of the tales on board is 'a youth' and we hear nothing of seasickness. It is implausible to identify his 'elder friend' with Thackeray, who was never a lawyer. No one has suggested a real-life original for the sanctimonious clergyman. The only person clearly recognisable behind the masks of the *Mari Magno* voyagers is the returning American – James Russell Lowell, who during the crossing struck up a lasting friendship with Clough. However, several episodes in the narrative recapitulate events of the 1852 voyage: a near-collision with Cape Race, and a fog in Halifax, for instance.

Each of the four major stories of the suite contains autobiographical echoes, and in each case the reference seems to be to a real or fantasised love affair in the poet's life.

The hero of the lawyer's first tale, spending a holiday, at twelve years of age, with a clerical uncle, is invited across the mountains to stay with six third cousins at a vicarage in Beaumaris. Arthur himself, at the age of ten, spent his first summer holidays between a widower clerical uncle in Mold, and a cousin by marriage, Dr Richard Howard, the vicar of Beaumaris. The hero has a juvenile flirtation with Emily, one of the Beaumaris daughters, and five years later pays further visits to the family, who have now moved inland; the romance does not prosper, as the hero boasts of too much school and college learning. The Howard family moved inland to Rhualissa, where Clough visited them from Oxford; in his diaries of 1841 he speaks, in code, of his 'Rhualissa enslavement' and mentions a 'Dora' with whom he feels he may have been foolish. Is it possible that Dora Howard is the Emily of the poem, and that the young Arthur had a fruitless juvenile passion for her?

We can be less hesitant about identifying the Emma of the clergyman's first tale. Clough spent the early summer of 1844 at Grasmere, near the Arnold family home at Fox How, and later in the year wrote a poem beginning 'When panting sighs the bosom fill', discussing whether it was possible to distinguish between passion, admiration, and reason. The poem, he confessed to a friend, was an expression of a personal dilemma. In 1846 he wrote to his sister about a lady whom she met at Ambleside whom he had hopes of marrying. This lady was most probably Jane Arnold, Matthew Arnold's eldest sister. Many elements in the Edmund and Emma story resemble features of the relationship between Arthur and Jane. Edmund and Arthur are each a couple of years older than the women; Edmund and Emma spend summers together near Wordsworth's wishing-gate adjacent to Fox How; Emma was sensitive to the unauthorised use of her Christian name, just as was the lady whom Arthur wrote to Annie about in 1846. Edmund, at 22, utters some verses that were written by Clough when he was visiting Fox How at 22 and, according to his diary, was 'very foolish'. Such coincidences suggest that Emma of the wishing-gate is Jane of Fox How. To be sure, in the poem Edmund eventually, and improbably, marries Emma, whereas if Arthur ever proposed to Jane he was rejected. But what Edmund finds in marriage – that love is fellow-service – is just what Clough was looking for in 1846 when he wrote to his sister 'it is not everyone who would like to be an helpmate in the business I am likely to have'.

Many readers have seen a further autobiographical element in the story that Clough was composing in his very last days, the lawyer's second tale. The theme of love for a Highland lassie, cutting across class barriers, is a frequent one in Clough's verse. It appears, for instance, in *The Bothie*, where the hero Philip falls in love with a crofter's daughter and takes her off to New Zealand. It is, I suppose, just possible that Clough seduced a servant girl after one of his Scottish reading parties, and if so there is something touching about his anxiety to complete, with his dying breath, a story in which a wife is reconciled with her husband's earlier mistress. However, there is no real evidence for any Scottish affair, still less for an intention to turn it into a marriage.

There is, however, some indication that Clough did need his wife's absolution for a more recent sin. This appears if we compare the letters that he wrote during his separation in France with the story told in the clergyman's second tale. His letters to his wife of 23 July (from Mont-Dore) and 30 July (from Bagnères-de-Luchon), proposing an early return home, show that he was at that time in exactly the same condition as Edward in the tale. Edward, while travelling abroad alone for his health's sake, is staying at a watering place and utterly bored. He writes to his wife suggesting that he should go home and resume his work. Emma replies that it is far too soon for him to return. On 26 July Blanche wrote to

Arthur, 'Why on earth you should come back in September I don't see.' He yielded to her pressure, and asked for an extension of his sick-leave. In the poem, Edward likewise yields, but shortly afterwards he has an adulterous affair. Three days later a letter comes from his wife enclosing one from his little daughter, 'in her large hand'. Just such a letter from his daughter Florence is pasted into Clough's letter book about this time.

Four days after his fall Edward writes to his wife and confesses his adultery. No such letter from Clough survives. But in his letter of 30 July to Blanche from Luchon he complains that it is not easily endurable 'to stay poking about abroad for more than two or three months at a time, all by oneself or something no better or perhaps worse'.

If by any chance Clough did have an affair with a fellow guest during his last days at Mont-Dore, this would explain the puzzling aspects of 'My Tale'. The journey recorded there would have occurred immediately after he had, in his own mind, shattered a marriage that had begun so happily. All that he is left with are the banal shards of solitary life and chance companionship that are described in 'My Tale'. Clough's journey from Mont-Dore to Bagnères would be one and the same as that of the remorseful Edward in the clergyman's second tale, which ended with a passing traveller being put down, haggard and in disarray.

We know that when Clough wrote the poem and read it aloud to the Tennysons, some weeks later, he broke down in tears. The poem and its conclusion may be aimed at persuading himself, as much as anyone else, that adultery need not be an end to a marriage – at a moment when his own marriage had just produced a new baby. However, given Clough's hypersensitive conscience, it is no easier here than in the case of the other autobiographical echoes in *Mari Magno* to decide whether he was recounting real or merely fantasised affairs.

6. The manuscripts and editions of *Mari Magno*

Manuscript versions of most of the tales are to be found in the 1861 diary that Clough took with him both on his Mediterranean trip in the spring and his Pyrenean trip in the fall of that year. It appears that he wrote daily entries into the diary between April and October and filled the blank pages with drafts of poems. There are also fair copies of the tales, in notebooks now preserved in the Bodleian library. The principal one is labelled MS Eng. Poet. d.145, which contains the entire suite of poems except for the officer's tale and the lawyer's second tale. The texts of the latter are to be found in two further Bodleian notebooks, MS Eng. Poet. d.147 and MS Eng. Poet. d.148.

When Blanche Clough produced the first edition of Clough's poems in 1862 she printed *Mari Magno* only in part. The Preface was followed by 'Edmund and Emma' renamed 'The Lawyer's Tale', 'My Tale', and 'Edward and Jane'. This decision, as she came to realise, was disastrous. The edition omitted two of the best poems, and the change of the titles of the others ruined the poet's careful characterisation of the distinct narrators. In a later version of the poems in 1863 and in the *Poems and Prose Remains* of 1869 Blanche published a much fuller version, containing all the tales in the MSS except the American's tale and the officer's tale. She made a number of emendations to the text and omitted a number of passages. The 1869 edition was reprinted fourteen times in the reign of Victoria, and went out of print only in 1932.

A scholarly edition of *Mari Magno* was made in 1951 by H.F. Lowry, A.L.P. Norrington and F.L. Mulhauser, in their volume *The Poems of Arthur Hugh Clough*. It was reprinted in the second edition of that work, edited by Mulhauser, which was published by the Clarendon Press in 1974. Anyone who works on Clough's poems owes an enormous debt to that edition, which presents a text which often differs from that published by Blanche, and which supplies an immense amount of information about manuscript readings and variants.

None the less, in this edition I have elected to follow, in general, the edition of 1869, Blanche's definitive text. The principal reason for this is that every piece of evidence about Clough's intentions that we possess was available to Blanche, and in addition she had had the experience of living and talking with her husband while he was working on the text. Most of the many minor changes that she made to the MSS are undoubted improvements, whether in scansion, syntax, clarity or consistency. They are the kind of revision that Clough himself would be likely to have made if he had lived to edit his own text. Where Clough's MSS offer variants, Blanche's choice between his first and his second thoughts seems to me often better than that of later editors.

It is not so easy to make a judgement about Blanche's omissions, whether of complete tales (the American's tale and the officer's tale) or of individual passages in a tale. The omissions seem to me to be of two kinds: some are on the basis of literary judgement, others on the basis of propriety. The Oxford editors suggest that the American's tale was omitted *pro pudore*; possibly so, but it would not be unreasonable to judge that by the time Clough had written the full series of longer poems he would no longer have thought such a flimsy piece worthy to stand beside them. I considered following Blanche's example, but have been persuaded by wiser heads that that would be a mistake. The officer's tale was omitted by Blanche on the grounds that it was incomplete. Here I think she was in error: the abrupt ending of the tale fits the bluff style of the narrator perfectly. Accordingly, I have printed it as reconstructed from the surviving MSS fragments.

The policy that I have adopted with regard to the individual omissions is this. Where Blanche's omission appeared to be made on literary grounds, I have followed her edition, but given the omitted passage in a footnote. Where, on the other hand, the omission seems to have been dictated by a Victorian sensibility that we no longer share, I have printed the text as in the MS, noting in a footnote that it does not appear in the 1869 edition.

I am greatly indebted to Philip Stewart, not only for the information contained in his published articles ('Has the poet told us his secret?', *The Oxford Magazine*, Michaelmas Term, 2003, pp. 5–8, and 'Arthur Hugh Clough's Last Summer', *Victorian Poetry*, summer 2013, 201–26), but also for many helpful discussions over the years. I am also indebted to P.J. Phelan, Tim Wilson and Jon Whitely for elucidating obscure allusions in the text. I am also grateful to Jill Paton Walsh and to my wife Nancy Kenny for comments on the introduction to this edition.

Anthony Kenny
December 2013

EASTER DAY
Naples, 1849

Through the great sinful streets of Naples as I past,
  With fiercer heat than flamed above my head
My heart was hot within me; till at last
  My brain was lightened when my tongue had said –
    Christ is not risen!

    Christ is not risen, no –
      He lies and moulders low;
    Christ is not risen!

What though the stone were rolled away, and though
    The grave found empty there? –   10
    If not there, then elsewhere;
If not where Joseph laid Him first, why then
    Where other men
Translaid Him after; in some humbler clay
    Long ere to-day
Corruption that sad perfect work hath done,
Which here she scarcely, lightly had begun.
    The foul engendered worm
Feeds on the flesh of the life-giving form
Of our most Holy and Anointed One.   20
    He is not risen, no –
    He lies and moulders low;
      Christ is not risen!

What if the women, ere the dawn was grey,
Saw one or more great angels, as they say,

Angels, or Him himself? Yet neither there, nor then,
Nor afterwards, nor elsewhere, nor at all,
Hath He appeared to Peter or the Ten,
Nor, save in thunderous terror, to blind Saul;
Save in an after-Gospel and late Creed,   30
      He is not risen indeed,
        Christ is not risen!

Or what if e'en, as runs the tale, the Ten
Saw, heard, and touched, again and yet again?
What if at Emmaus' inn, and by Capernaum's lake,
      Came One the bread that brake,
Came One that spake as never mortal spake,
And with them ate, and drank, and stood, and walked about?
      Ah! 'some' did well to 'doubt'!
Ah! the true Christ, while these things came to pass,   40
Nor heard, nor spake, nor walked, nor lived, alas!
      He was not risen, no –
      He lay and mouldered low,
        Christ was not risen!

As circulates in some great city crowd
A rumour changeful, vague, importunate, and loud,
From no determinate centre, or of fact,
      Or authorship exact,
      Which no man can deny
        Nor verify;   50
So spread the wondrous fame;
      He all the same
Lay senseless, mouldering, low.
He was not risen, no –
      Christ was not risen!

Ashes to ashes, dust to dust;
As of the unjust, also of the just –
      Yea, of that Just One, too!

This is the one sad Gospel that is true –
   Christ is not risen!   60

Is He not risen, and shall we not rise?
   Oh, we unwise!
What did we dream, what wake we to discover?
Ye hills, fall on us, and ye mountains, cover!
   In darkness and great gloom
Come ere we thought it is *our* day of doom,
From the cursed world which is one tomb,
   Christ is not risen!

Eat, drink, and play, and think that this is bliss!
There is no heaven but this,   70
   There is no hell,
Save earth, which serves the purpose doubly well,
   Seeing it visits still
With equalest apportionment of ill
Both good and bad alike, and brings to one same dust
   The unjust and the just
   With Christ, who is not risen.

Eat, drink, and die, for we are souls bereaved,
 Of all the creatures under heaven's wide cope
  We are most hopeless, who had once most hope,   80
And most beliefless, that had most believed.
   Ashes to ashes, dust to dust
   As of the unjust, also of the just –
   Yea, of that Just One too!
   It is the one sad Gospel that is true –
   Christ is not risen!

   Weep not beside the tomb,
   Ye women, unto whom
He was great solace while ye tended Him;
   Ye who with napkin o'er the head   90

And folds of linen round each wounded limb
      Laid out the Sacred Dead;
And thou that bar'st Him in thy wondering womb;
Yea, Daughters of Jerusalem, depart,
Bind up as best ye may your own sad bleeding heart:
Go to your homes, your living children tend,
      Your earthly spouses love;
      Set your affections *not* on things above,
Which moth and rust corrupt, which quickliest come to end:
Or pray, if pray ye must, and pray, if pray ye can,   100
For death; since dead is He whom ye deemed more than man,
      Who is not risen, no –
      But lies and moulders low,
        Who is not risen!

      Ye men of Galilee!
Why stand ye looking up to heaven, where Him ye ne'er may see,
Neither ascending hence, nor hither returning again?
      Ye ignorant and idle fishermen!
Hence to your huts, and boats, and inland native shore,
      And catch not men, but fish;   110
      Whate'er things ye might wish
Him neither here nor there ye e'er shall meet with more.
      Ye poor deluded youths, go home,
      Mend the old nets ye left to roam,
      Tie the split oar, patch the torn sail:
      It was indeed 'an idle tale' –
        He was not risen!

And oh, good men of ages yet to be,
Who shall believe *because* ye did not see,
      Oh, be ye warned, be wise!   120
      No more with pleading eyes,
      And sobs of strong desire,
      Unto the empty vacant void aspire,
Seeking another and impossible birth

That is not of your own, and only mother earth.
But if there is no other life for you,
Sit down and be content, since this must even do:
       He is not risen.

      One look, and then depart,
        Ye humble and ye holy men of heart;   130
And ye! ye ministers and stewards of a Word
Which ye would preach, because another heard, –
       Ye worshippers of that ye do not know,
      Take these things hence and go:
       He is not risen!

      Here on our Easter Day
We rise, we come, and lo! we find Him not,
Gardener nor other, on the sacred spot:
Where they have laid Him there is none to say;
No sound, nor in, nor out – no word   140
Of where to seek the dead or meet the living Lord.
There is no glistering of an angel's wings,
There is no voice of heavenly clear behest:
Let us go hence and think upon these things
      In silence, which is best.
      Is He not risen? No –
      But lies and moulders low,
       Christ is not risen.

DIPSYCHUS

ACT I

Scene 1: The Piazza at Venice, 9 pm[1]

Dipsychus
The Scene is different and the Place, the air
Tastes of the nearer north; the people too
Not perfect southern lightness. Wherefore then
Should those old verses come into my mind
I made last year at Naples? O poor fool,   5
Still nesting on thyself. –

'Through the great sinful streets of Naples as I past
With fiercer heat than flamed above my head
My heart was hot within; the fire burnt, and at last
My brain was lightened when my tongue had said,   10
        Christ is not risen!'

Spirit
        Christ is not risen? Oh indeed!
        I didn't know that was your creed.

Di.
So it goes on. Too lengthy to repeat
        'Christ is not risen'   15

Sp.
        Dear, how odd!
        He'll tell us next there is no God.

1   The Piazza San Marco, the central square of Venice.

Dipsychus

I thought 'twas in the Bible plain,
On the third day he rose again.

Di.

'Ashes to Ashes, Dust to Dust
As of the Unjust also of the Just –   20
       Yea, of that Just One too!
Is He not risen and shall we not rise?
       O we unwise'

Sp.

Well, now it's anything but clear
What is the tone that's taken here.   25
What is your logic? What's your theology?
Is it or is it not neology?[2]
That's a great fault; you're this and that,
And here and there, and nothing flat.
Yet writing's golden word, what is it   30
But the three syllables 'explicit'?
Say, if you cannot help it, less,
But what you do put, put express.
I fear that rule won't meet your feeling;
You think half-showing, half-concealing,   35
Is God's own method of revealing.

Di.
To please my own poor mind; to find repose
To physic the sick soul; to furnish vent
To diseased humours in the moral frame.

Sp.

Hm! and the tone then after all   40
       Something of the ironical?
Sarcastic say; or were it fitter
To style it the religious bitter?

2   Modernising theology of a critical tendency.

Dipsychus

Di.
Interpret it I cannot. I but wrote it.

Sp.

Perhaps; but none that read can doubt it   45
There is a strong Strauss-smell about it.[3]
Heavens! at your years your time to fritter
Upon a critical hair-splitter!
Take larger views (and quit your Germans)
From the Analogy and Sermons;[4]   50
I fancied – you must doubtless know –
Butler had proved an age ago
That in religious as profane things
'Twas useless trying to explain things.
Men's business-wits, the only sane things,   55
These and compliance are the main things
God, Revelation and the rest of it,
Bad at the best, we make the best of it.
Not quite the things we chose to think;
But neither is the world rose pink.   60
Yet *it* is fact as plain as day;
So may the rest be; who can say?
Thus life we see is wondrous odd
And so, we argue, may be God.
By heaven I don't explain the thing   65
But by the Father and the Son
And Holy Ghost which all are one
And by the Apostles' holy pen
And all the common sense of men,
This Puritano-Pantheistic   70
Mush of Neologist and Mystic

---

3   D.F. Strauss's *Life of Jesus*, translated by George Eliot in 1846, treated the Gospels as mythical.

4   Works of the eighteenth-century Anglican Bishop Butler, recommended to Clough by the Provost of Oriel some years earlier as a great antidote to unbelief.

8

Is, of all doctrines, the least reasonable
Why should you fancy you know more of it
Than all the old folks that thought before of it
Like a good subject and wise man,   75
Believe whatever things you can.
Take your religion as 'twas found you
And say no more of it – confound you.

Di.
Interpret it I cannot. I but wrote it
At Naples, truly, as the preface tells,   80
Last year in the Toledo;[5] it came on me,
And did me good at once. At Naples then,
At Venice now. Ah! and I think at Venice
Christ is not risen either.

Sp.
                    Nay –
          'Twas well enough once in a way   85
          Such things don't fall out every day
          Having once happened, as we know
          In Palestine so long ago
          How should it now in Venice here?
          Where people, true enough, appear   90
          To appreciate more and understand
          Their ices, and their Austrian band,
          And dark-eyed girls than what occurred
          So long ago to the Eternal Word.
          Look at them now –

Di.
                    The whole great square they fill   95
From the red flaunting streamers on the staffs
And that barbaric portal of St Mark's

5   The main artery of Naples, opened in 1570 by the Viceroy Don Pedro di Toledo.
     Now the Via Roma.

To where, unnoticed, at the darker end,
I sit upon my step. One great grey crowd.
The Campanile to the silent stars   100
Goes up above – its apex lost in air.
While these – do what?

Sp.

          Enjoy the minute,
And the substantial blessing in it:
Ices, *par exemple*; evening air
Some pretty faces here and there;   105
And all the sweets in perfect plenty
Of the old *dolce far niente*.[6]
Music! Up, up; it isn't fit
With beggars here on steps to sit.
Up to the café! Take a chair   110
And join the wiser idlers there.
Aye! what a crowd! and what a noise!
With all these screaming half-breeched boys.
Partout dogs, boys, and women wander –
And see that fellow singing yonder;   115
Singing, ye gods, and dancing too –
Tooraloo tooraloo tooraloo loo
Fiddle di diddle di diddle di da
Figaro su, Figaro giù
Figaro qua, Figaro là[7]   120
How he likes doing it! ha ha!

Di.
While these do what – ah heaven!

Sp.

          If you want to pray
I'll step aside a little way

6   'Sweet idleness'.
7   From the *Largo al Factotum* in Rossini's *Barber of Seville*.

I go, but will not be far gone;   125
You may be wanting me anon.
Our lonely pious altitudes
Are followed quick by prettier moods.
Who knows not with what ease devotion
Slips into earthlier emotion?

Di.
While these do what? Ah heaven, too true, at Venice   130
Christ is not risen either!

Scene 2: The Public Garden[1]

Di.
Assuredly a lively scene!
And, ah, how pleasant, something green!
With circling heavens one perfect rose
Each smoother patch of water grows,
Hence to where, o'er the full tide's face, 5
We see the Palace and the Place
And the White Dome.[2] Beauteous but hot.
Where in the meantime is the spot
My favourite, where by masses blue
And white cloud-folds, I follow true 10
The great Alps, rounding grandly o'er
Huge arc, to the Dalmatian shore?

Sp.
        This rather stupid place to-day
        'Tis true, is most extremely gay,
        And rightly – the Assunzione 15
        Was always a *gran' funzione*.[3]

---

1   The Giardini Pubblici, created on the orders of Napoleon in 1807, remain the
    largest public green spaces in Venice, in the south-east corner of the city.
2   The Doge's palace, the Piazza San Marco, and the church of Santa Maria della
    Salute, at the entrance to the Grand Canal, are all visible from the entrance to
    the Giardini, now a *vaporetto* stop.
3   'A great occasion'. The feast of the Assumption of the Blessed Virgin Mary, 15
    August, is of both internal and external significance for the poem. The feast is
    a celebration of the etherialisation of female flesh, which presents a contrast
    with the carnality of Dipsychus's temptation. But 15 August 1850, besides being
    the dramatic date of the scene, was a day of great importance in Clough's
    personal life: it was the wedding day of Jane Arnold (Matthew's sister) whom
    Clough had hoped in vain to marry.

Di.

What is this persecuting voice that haunts me?
Where? Whence? Of whom? How am I to detect?
Myself or not myself? My own bad thoughts,
Or some external agency at work,   20
To lead me who knows whither?

Sp.

                         Eh?
            We're certainly in luck to-day
            What lots of boats before us plying –
            Gay parties, singing, shouting, crying
            Saluting others past them flying!   25
            What numbers at the landing lying!
            With lots of pretty girls too, hieing
            Hither and thither – coming, going
            And with what satisfaction showing
            To our male eyes unveiled and bare   30
            Their dark exuberance of hair,
            Black eyes, rich tints, and sundry graces
            Of classic pure Italian faces!

Di.

Off, off! Oh heaven, depart, depart, depart!
Oh me! The toad sly-sitting at Eve's ear[4]   35
Whispered no dream more poisonous than this!

Sp.

            A perfect show of girls I see it is
            Ah, what a charming foot, ye deities!
            In that attraction as one fancies
            Italy's not so rich as France is;   40
            In Paris –

---

4   In Milton's *Paradise Lost* (IV, 800) Satan is found 'squat, like a toad, close at the
     ear of Eve'

Di.

                    Cease, cease, cease!
I will not hear this. Leave me!

Sp.

                    So!
How do those pretty verses go?

> *Ah comme je regrette*
> *Mon bras si dodu*   45
> *Ma jambe bien faite*
> *Et le temps perdu!*
> *Et le temps perdu!*[5]

'Tis here, I see, the custom too
For damsels eager to be lovered   50
To go about with arms uncovered;
And doubtless there's a special charm
In looking at a well-shaped arm.
In Paris, I was saying –

Di.

                    Ah me, me!
Clear stars above, thou roseate westward sky,   55
Take up my being into yours; assume
My sense to own you only; steep my brain
In your essential purity. Or, great Alps,
That wrapping round your heads in solemn clouds
Seem sternly to sweep past our vanities,   60
Lead me with you – take me away; preserve me!
– Ah, if it must be, look then, foolish eyes –
Listen fond ears; but oh, poor mind, stand fast!

---

5   A slightly garbled version of a poem by the ribald French poet Béranger, long
     a favourite with Clough and Arnold. 'How I miss my fine plump arm and my
     well shaped leg and the times gone by'.

Sp.

        In Paris, at the Opera
        In the *coulisses*[6] – but ah, aha!   65
        There was a glance, I saw you spy it –
        So shall we follow suit and try it?
        Pooh, what a goose you are! quick, quick!
        This hesitation makes me sick
        You simpleton! What's your alarm?   70
        She'd merely thank you for your arm.

Di.

Sweet thing! ah well! but yet I am not sure
Ah no, I think she did not mean it. No.

Sp.

        Plainly, unless I much mistake
        She likes a something in your make: 75
        She turned her head – another glance –
        She really gives you every chance.

Di.

Ah pretty thing – well, well. Yet should I go?
Alas, I cannot say. What should I do?

Sp.

        What should you do? Well that is funny!   80
        I think you are supplied with money.

Di.

No, no – it may not be. I could, I would –
And yet I would not – cannot. To what end?

Sp.

        A servant girl, by the Eternal,

6   'Behind the scenes'.

O'er took by something over-vernal[7]   85
The very thing, my boy, for you
She'll teach you quickly what to do.
Her fellow Nurse would egg her on.
But she – she blushes. Ah, they're gone.
A most uncommon chance I swear   90
As sweet a little thing as e'er
I saw since first I learnt to stare
And to repulse her in that fashion
O God – I'm all but mad with passion.
Well, well, it's too late now – they're gone;   95
Some wiser youth is coming on.

7   A more than spring-like erotic impulse.

Scene 3: The Quays

Di.
O hateful, hateful, hateful! To the Hotel!

Sp.
>   Pooh, what the devil! What's the harm?
>   I merely bid you take her arm.

Di.
And I half yielded! O unthinking I!
O weak weak fool! O God how quietly   5
Out of our better into our worse selves
Out of a true world which our reason knew
Into a false world which our fancy makes
We pass and never know – O weak weak fool.

Sp.
>   Well, if you don't wish, why, you don't.   10
>   Leave it! But that's just what you won't.
>   Come now! How many times per diem
>   Are you not hankering to try 'em?

Di.
O moon and stars forgive! And thou clear heaven
Look pureness back into me. O great God,   15
Why, why in wisdom and in grace's name,
And in the name of saints and saintly thoughts,
Of mothers, and of sisters, and chaste wives,
And angel woman-faces we have seen,
And angel woman-spirits we have guessed,   20
And innocent sweet children, and pure love,
Why did I ever one brief moment's space

To this insidious lewdness lend chaste ears,
Or parley with this filthy Belial?[1]
O were it that vile questioner that loves   25
To thrust his fingers into right and wrong
And before proof knows nothing – or the fear
Of being behind the world – which is, the wicked.

Sp.

        O yes, you dream of sin and shame –
        Trust me, it leaves one much the same   30
        'Tisn't Elysium[2] any more
        Than what comes after or before:
        But heavens! as innocent a thing
        As picking strawberries in spring.
        You think I'm anxious to allure you –   35
        My object is much more to cure you.
        With the high amatory-poetic
        My temper's no way sympathetic;
        To play your pretty woman's fool
        I hold but fit for boys from school.   40
        I know it's mainly your temptation
        To think the thing a revelation
        A mystic mouthful that will give
        Knowledge and death – none know and live!
        I tell you plainly that it brings   45
        Some ease; but the emptiness of things
        (That one old sermon Earth still preaches
        Until we practise what she teaches)
        Is the sole lesson you'll learn by it.
        Still you undoubtedly should try it.   50
        'Try all things' bad and good, no matter;

---

1   In *Paradise Lost* Belial is one of Satan's colleagues, particularly associated with
    unchastity: a devil 'than whom a spirit more lewd fell not from heaven' (I, 490).
2   In Greek mythology the Elysian fields were the paradisal abode of heroes after
    their death.

You can't till then hold fast the latter.
If not, this itch will stick and vex you
Your live long days till death unsex you –
Hide in your bones, for aught I know,   55
And with you to the next world go.
Briefly – you cannot rest, I'm certain
Until your hand has drawn the curtain.
Once known the little lies behind it,
You'll go your way and never mind it.   60
Ill's only cure is, never doubt it,
To do – and think no more about it.[3]

Di.
Strange talk, strange words. Ah me, I cannot say.
Can I believe it even of us men
That once the young exuberance drawn off   65
The liquor would run clear; that once appeased
The vile inquisitive wish, brute appetite fed,
The very void that ebbing flood had left
From purer sources would be now refilled
That to rank weeds of rain spring mowed off   70
Would a green wholesome aftermath succeed;
That the empty garnished tenement of the soul
Would not behold the seven replace the one:[4]
Could I indeed as of some men I might
Think this of maidens also? But I know;   75
Not as the male is, is the female. Eve
Was moulded not as Adam.

---

3   An anticipation of Oscar Wilde's dictum 'The only way to get rid of a tempta-
    tion is to yield to it'.
4   Mt 12, 43–45: 'When the unclean spirit is gone out of a man, he walketh through
    dry places, seeking rest, and findeth none. Then goeth he, and taketh with
    himself seven other spirits more wicked than himself, and they enter in and
    dwell there: and the last state of the man is worse than the first.'

Sp.

             Stuff!
The women like it; that's enough.
The pretty creatures come and proffer
The measures of their privy coffer   80
And I refuse not a good offer
Sold in the shambles without question
I eat, and vex not my digestion.

Di.

Could I believe, as of a man I might,
So a good girl from weary workday hours   85
And from the long monotony of toil
Might safely purchase these wild intervals,
And from that banquet rise refreshed, and wake
And shake her locks and as before go forth
Invigorate, unvitiate to the task –   90
But no, it is not so.

Sp.

           That may be true
It is uncommon, though some do.
In married life you sometimes find
Proceedings something of the kind
Yet single women, ah *mon Dieu*   95
Being women, must have much ado
Not to o'erstep the *juste milieu*.

Di.

No, no, apart from pressure of the world
And yearning sensibilities of soul,
The swallowed dram entails the drunkard's curse   100
Of burnings ever new; and the coy girl
Turns to the flagrant woman of the street,
Ogling for hirers, horrible to see.

Sp.

>This is the high moral way of talking
>I'm well aware about street-walking.   105

Di.

Hungering but without appetite; athirst
From impotence; no humblest feeling left
Of all that once too rank exuberance.
No kindly longing, no sly coyness now
Not e'en the elastic appetence of lust   110
Not a poor petal hanging to that stalk
Where thousands once were redolent and rich.
Look, she would fain allure; but she is cold,
The ripe lips paled, the frolick pulses stilled,
The quick eye dead, the once fair flushing cheek   115
Flaccid under its paint; the once heaving bosom –
Ask not! for oh, the sweet bloom of desire
In hot fruition's pawey fingers turns
To dullness and the deadly spreading spot
Of rottenness inevitably soon   120
That while we hold, we hate. Sweet Peace! No more!

Sp.

>Fiddle di diddle, fal lal lal!
>By candlelight they are *pas mal*
>Better and worse, of course, there are:
>Star differs (with the price) from star.[5]   125
>I found it hard I must confess
>To a small Frenchman to say yes
>Who told me, in a steamer talking
>That one can pick up in one's walking
>In the Strand Street in London town   130

---

5   St Paul, discussing the final resurrection, compares the status of a risen body
    to the glory of the stars, and adds 'one star differeth from another in glory'
    (I. Cor. 15, 41).

Something quite nice for half a crown
But – in the dark what comes amiss?
Except bad breath and syphilis.

Di.
Could I believe that any child of Eve
Were formed and fashioned, raised and reared for nought   135
But to be swilled with animal delight
And yield five minutes' pleasure to the male –
Could I think cherry lips and chubby cheeks
That seem to exist express for such fond play,
Hold in suppression nought to come; o'ershell   140
No lurking virtuality of more –

Sp.
It was a lover and his lass
    With a hey and a ho and a hey nonino!
Betwixt the acres of the rye,
    With a hey and a ho and a hey nonino! 145
These pretty country folks would lie –
    In the spring time, the pretty spring time.[6]

Di.
And could I think I owed it not to her,
In virtue of our manhood's stronger sight,
Even against entreaty to forbear –   150

Sp.
O Joseph and Don Quixote![7] This
A chivalry of chasteness is,

6   An abbreviated version of the song in Shakespeare's *As You Like It*, Act V
    Scene 3.
7   Joseph may be either the Old Testament patriarch who resisted the advances
    of Potiphar's wife in Genesis 39, or the husband of the Virgin Mary. Don
    Quixote, in Cervantes' novel, makes a peasant girl, Dulcinea, the queen of his
    heart, but his amorous attentions never get beyond his own imagination.

That turns to nothing all that story
Has made out of your ancient glory!
Still I must urge that, though 'tis sad,   155
'Tis sure, once gone, for good or bad
The prize whose loss we are deploring
Is physically past restoring;
C'en est fait.[8] Nor can God's own self,
As Coleridge on the dusty shelf   160
Says in his wicked Omniana,
Restore to Ina frail or Ana
Her once rent *hymenis membrana.*[9]
So that it needs consideration
By what more moral occupation   165
To support this vast population.

Di.
Could I believe that purity were not
Lodg'd somewhere, precious pearl, e'en underneath
The hardest coarsest outside; could I think
That any heart in women's bosom set   170
By tenderness o'ermastering mean desire
Faithfulness, love, were unredeemable,
Or could I think it sufferable in me
For my poor pleasure's sake to superadd
One possible finger's pressure to the weight   175
That turns, and grinds as in a fierce machine
This hapless kind, these pariahs of the sex –

Sp.
Well, people talk – their sentimentality.
Meantime, as by some fatality

8   'It's all over'.
9   Coleridge in *Omniana*, a collection of jottings, refers to the *De Divina Omnipotentia* of the medieval theologian St Peter Damiani which discusses the question whether God can restore virginity to a non-virgin. 'Ina' and 'Ana' are typical endings of Italian female forenames.

Mortality is still mortality   180
Nor has corruption, spite of facility,
And doctrines of perfectibility
Yet put on incorruptibility.
As women are and the world goes
They're not so badly off – who knows?   185
They die, as we do in the end;
They marry – or they *superintend*;[10]
Or Sidney Herberts sometimes rise,
And send them out to colonise.[11]

Di.
Or could I think that it had been for nought   190
That from my boyhood until now, in spite
Of most misguiding theories, at the moment
Somewhat has ever stepped in to arrest
My ingress at the fatal-closing door,
That many and many a time my foolish foot   195
O'ertreading the dim sill, spite of itself
And spite of me, instinctively fell back.

Sp.
Like Balaam's ass,[12] in spite of thwacking
Against the wall his master backing
Because of something hazy stalking   200
Just in the way they should be walking –
Soon after too, he took to talking!

10 I.e. become a madam in a brothel.
11 In 1849 Herbert and his wife founded the Female Emigration Fund to assist
    women to emigrate to the colonies so that they could marry and breed a white
    population there.
12 Balaam, riding on his ass in a direction displeasing to God, found an angel
    blocking his way. The ass refused to go further, and was given a severe beating.
    God thereupon empowered the ass to speak in rebuke of Balaam (Num. 22,
    20–34).

24

Di.
Backed, and refused my bidding – Could I think
In spite of carnal understanding's sneers
All this fortuitous only – all a chance?   205

Sp.
   Ah, just what I was going to say
   An Angel met you in the way
   Cry mercy of his heavenly highness
   I took him for that cunning shyness.

Di.
Shyness. 'Tis but another word for shame;   210
And that for sacred instinct. Off ill thoughts!
'Tis holy ground your foot has stepped upon.

Sp.
   Ho, Virtue quotha![13] Trust who knows
   There's not a girl that by us goes
   But mightn't have you if she chose: 215
   No doubt but you would give her trouble;
   But then you'd pay her for it double.
   By Jove – if I were but a lass,
   I'd soon see what I'd bring to pass.

Di.
O welcome then the sweet domestic bonds   220
The matrimonial sanctities, the hopes
And cares of wedded life; parental thoughts,
The prattle of young children, the good word
Of fellow men, the sanction of the law,
And permanence and habit, that transmute   225
Grossness itself to crystal. O why why

---

13 'Says he'.

Why ever let this speculating brain
Rest upon other objects than on this?

Sp.

> Well, well – if you must stick perforce
> Unto the ancient holy course   230
> And map your life out on the plan
> Of the connubial puritan;
> For God's sake carry out your creed,
> Go home, and marry, – and be d—d.[14]
> I'll help you.

Di.

> You!

Sp.

> O never scout me: 235
> I know you'll ne'er propose without me.

Di.

Marry, ah yes that is a question
Indeed 'tis useless thinking now of that.
Meantime that sweet girl – I see her in my mind
Step forward – blush – and turn and look behind.   240
Shall we not take another turn, Mephisto,
May we not meet her yet –

Sp.

> O Christ,
> I thought your worship would come to.
> Yes, yes, a little quiet turn
> By all means let us live and learn   245
> Here's many a lady still waylaying
> And sundry gentlemen purveying.
> And if 'twere only just to see

14 'D—d' is of course a euphemism for 'damned'; but it could be pronounced
   'deed', just as we talk of someone having 'peed' as a euphemism for 'pissed'.

26

The room of an Italian *fille*
'Twere worth the trouble and the money   250
You'll like to find – I found it funny –
The chamber *où vous faites votre affaire*[15]
Stands nicely fitted up for prayer.
While dim you trace along one end
The Sacred Supper's length extend   255
The calm Madonna o'er your head
Smiles, *con bambino*,[16] on the bed
Where – but your chaste ears I must spare
Where, as we said, *vous faites votre affaire.*
They'll suit you, these Venetian pets,   260
So natural, not the least coquettes,
Really at times one quite forgets –
Well, would you like perhaps to arrive at
A pretty creature's home in private?
We can look in, just say goodnight,   265
And if you like to stay, all right
Just as you fancy – is it well?

Di.
Oh heaven, to yield a treasured innocence
To frosty fondlings and a forced caress
To heavy kisses and the plastery speech   270
Of a would-be but can't be sentiment.

Sp.

You don't like sentiment? He he!
'T should have been you instead of me,
When t'other day just after noon
Having got up a little soon   275
Tiring of cafés, quays and barks
I turned for shade into St Mark's.
I sit a while studying mosaics

15 'Where you do your business'.
16 'With the baby Jesus'.

Which we unauthorised laics
Have leave to like – a girl slips by   280
And gives the signal with her eye.
She takes the door; I follow out:
Curious, amused, but scarce in doubt
While street on street she winds about
Heedful at corners, but *du reste*   285
Assured, and grandly self-possessed
Trips up a stairs at last, and lands me
Up with her petticoats, and hands me
Much as one might a *pot de chambre*
The vessel that relieves *le membre.*[17]   290
No would-be pretty hesitation
Most business-like in her vocation
She but the brief half-instant lingers
And strikes her bargain with five fingers
'Twas well enough – I do not mean   295
Voluptuous, but plain and clean;
Doctors perhaps might recommend it
You step and do the thing and end it.

Di.

Myself, I like a mild infusion
Of something bordering on illusion   300
To dream and dreaming know one knows
That as the dream comes, so it goes –
You know that feeling, I suppose
Foolish it may be, but it serves
One's purpose better for one's nerves.   305

Sp.

Well! the Piazza? *mio carino*[18]
A better place than the Giardino.

17 The spirit refers to the chamber pot and the male member in the decent obscu-
    rity of a foreign language.
18 'My dear young man'.

28

Scene 4: The Hotel

Sp.

O yes, that was a rare adventure
I took the pains to make you enter;
You saw the lady well undrest,
And wishing her a good night's rest
Went off because (you said) 'twas Sunday   5
You'd probably return on Monday.
I set you off to talk a bit
And thought you on the highway;
Lo and behold, after a space
Of cooing and billing   10
You turn and give her, going off
A sovereign for a shilling.

Di.

O hateful, hateful – let me shudder it off.
Thank God, thank God we are here – that's well at least.

Sp.

Well, well I may have been a little strong   15
Of course I wouldn't have you do what's wrong.
But we who've lived out in the world you know,
Don't see these little things precisely so.
You feel yourself, to shrink and yet be fain
And still to move and still draw back again   20
Is a proceeding wholly without end.
If the plebeian street don't suit my friend
Why, he must try the drawing room, one fancies,
And he shall run to concerts and to dances
And with my aid, go into good society.   25
Life little loves, 'tis true, this peevish piety;

E'en they with whom it thinks to be securest –
Your most religious, delicatest, purest –
Discern, and show as pious people can
Their feeling that you are not quite a man.   30
Still, the thing has its place; and with sagacity
Much might be done by one of your capacity.
A virtuous attachment formed judiciously
Would come, one sees, uncommonly propitiously:
Turn you but your affections the right way   35
And what mayn't happen none of us can say.
For in despite of devils and of mothers
Your good young men make catches, too, like others.
Oh yes, into society we go!
At worst, 'twill teach you much you ought to know.   40

Di.
To herd with people that one owns no care for
Friend it with strangers that one sees but once;
To drain the heart with endless complaisance;
To warp the unfashioned diction on the lip,
And twist one's mouth to counterfeit; enforce   45
Reluctant looks to falsehood; base-alloy
The ingenious golden frankness of the past;
To calculate and plot; be rough and smooth,
Forward and silent; deferential, cool,
Not by one's humour, which is the safe truth,   50
But on consideration!

Sp.
                    That is, act
Upon dispassionate judgement of the fact
Look all the data fairly in the face
And rule your conduct simply by the case.

Di.
On vile consideration. At the best   55

Dipsychus

With pallid hotbed courtesies forestall
The green and vernal spontaneity,
And waste the priceless moments of the man
In regulating manner. Whether these things
Be right, I do not know: I only know 'tis   60
To lose one's youth too early. Oh, not yet,
Not yet I make this sacrifice.

Sp.

                              Du tout!
To give up nature's just what wouldn't do.
By all means keep your sweet ingenuous graces,
And use them at the proper times and places.   65
For work, for play, for business, talk, and love,
I own as wisdom truly from above
The scripture of the serpent and the dove;[1]
Nor's aught so perfect for the world's affairs
As the old parable of wheat and tares;[2]   70
What we all love is good touched up by evil –
Religion's self must have a spice of devil.

Di.

                    Let it be enough
That in our needful mixture with the world,
On each new morning with the rising sun   75
Our rising heart, fresh from the seas of sleep,
Scarce o'er the level lifts his purer orb
Ere lost and sullied with polluting smoke –
A noonday coppery disk. Lo, scarce come forth

---

1   Jesus sent his disciples on their mission with the injunction 'Be ye wise as
    serpents, and harmless as doves' (Mt 10, 16).
2   In the parable a man sowed good seed in his field, but an enemy contaminated
    the field with tares, or weeds. The reapers were instructed to let weeds and
    wheat grow together until harvest time when they would be separated. The
    point of the parable is to explain the coexistence of good and evil in the world
    prior to the Last Judgement.

Some vagrant miscreant meets, and with a look   80
Transmutes me his, and for a whole sick day
Lepers me.

Sp.

      Why, the one thing, I assure you
From which good company can't but secure you.
About the individuals 't'ain't so clear
But who can doubt the general atmosphere?   85

Di.
Ay, truly, who at first? But in a while –

Sp.
O dear, this o'er discernment makes me smile.
Do you pretend to tell me you can see
Without one touch of melting sympathy
Those lovely, fragrant flowers, that fill with bloom   90
The brilliant season's gay *parterre*-like room,
Moving serene yet swiftly through the dances;
Those graceful forms and perfect countenances
Whose every fold and line in all their dresses
Something refined and exquisite expresses?   95
To see them smile and hear them talk so sweetly
In me destroys all grosser thoughts completely.
I really seem without exaggeration
To experience the True Regeneration.[3]
One's own dress too, one's manner, what one's doing   100
And saying, all assist to one's renewing.
I love to see, in these their fitting places
The bows, the forms, and all you call grimaces.
I heartily could wish we'd kept some more of them,

---

3   The true regeneration, according to evangelical Christianity, is the inward
    conviction of redemption; it is contrasted with the regeneration through the
    sacrament of Baptism in which Catholic Christians believed.

However much they talk about the bore of them.   105
Fact is, your awkward parvenus are shy at it
Afraid to look like waiters if they try at it.
'Tis sad to what democracy is leading;
Give me your Eighteenth Century for high breeding.
Though I can put up gladly with the present   110
And quite can think our modern parties pleasant.
One shouldn't analyse the thing too nearly;
The main effect is admirable, clearly.
Good manners, said our great aunts, next to piety;
And so, my friend, hurrah for good society.   115
For mind you, if you don't do this, you still
Have got to tell me what it is you will.

Scene 5

Sp.

> Insulted! by the living Lord!
> He laid his hand upon his sword.
> *Fort* did he say?[1] A German brute
> With neither heart nor brains to shoot.

Di.

What does he mean? He's wrong. I had done nothing.   5
'Twas a mistake – more his I am sure than mine.
He is quite wrong – I feel it. Come let us go.

Sp.

> Go up to him! – you must, that's flat.
> Be threatened by a beast like that!

Di.

He's violent: what can I do against him?   10
I neither wish to be killed or to kill:
What's more, I never yet have touched a sword,
Nor fired, but twice, a pistol in my life.

Sp.

> O, never mind, 'twon't come to fighting
> Only some verbal small requiting;   15
> Or give your card – we'll do't by writing.
> He'll not stick to it. Soldiers too
> Are cowards, just like me or you.
> What! not a single word to throw at

---

1   'Get out'. See later in the scene, lines 225–26.

This snarling dog of a d—d Croat?[2]   20

Di.
My heaven! Why should I care? he does not hurt me.
If he is wrong, it is the worse for him.
I certainly did nothing – I shall go.

Sp.
> Did nothing! I should think not; no,
> Nor ever will, I dare be sworn!   25
> But, O my friend, well-bred, well-born –
> You to behave so in these quarrels
> Makes me half doubtful of your morals!
>   It were all one
> You had been some shopkeeper's son   30
> Whose childhood ne'er was shown aught better
> Than bills of creditor and debtor.

Di.
By heaven, it falls from off me like the rain
From the oil-coat. I seem in spirit to see
How he and I at some great day shall meet   35
Before some awful judgement-seat of truth;
And I could deem that I behold him there
Come praying for the pardon I give now,
Did not I think these matters too, too small
For any record on the leaves of time.   40

Sp.
> O Lord! and walking with your sister
> If some foul brute stept up and kissed her,
> You'd leave that also, I dare say
> On account for the judgement day.

2   Since 1849 Venice had been occupied by Austrian troops, of which the main detachment was Kinsky's Croat regiment.

Di.
Oh, these skin-bites, these airy words   45
Which at the moment seem to pierce us through,
And one hour after are acknowledged nought;
These pricks of pride, these petty personal hurts,
O thou great Watcher of this noisy world,
What are they in thy sight? Or what in his   50
Who finds some end of Action in his life?
What e'en in those whose sole permitted course
Is to pursue his peaceful byway walk,
And live his brief life purely in Thy sight,
And righteously towards his brother-men?   55

Sp.
                    And whether, so you're just and fair
                    Other folks are so, you don't care
                    You who profess more love than others
                    For your poor sinful human brothers.
                    But this anon we'll come, my friend, to   60
                    My previous question first attend to.

Di.
For grosser evils their gross remedies
The laws afford us; let us be content.
For finer wounds the law would, if it could,
Find medicine too; it cannot, let us bear;   65
For sufferance is the badge of all men's tribes.
For these no code of delicatest enactment
No court of honour's subtlest precedents
No rules, no judges, can ensure defence
A wretched witling[3] with his hour of prate   70
Destroys my nascent thoughts: the infectious eyes
Of some poor misbegotten waif of clay
Breed scurvy in my peace. Say shall I draw

3   A man who makes feeble jokes.

36

This sword you love, to save myself from these,
Because a man is vulgar cut him down   75
And shoot a witling for an inept joke?

Sp.

        Because we can't do all we would
        Does it follow, to do nothing's good?
        No way to help the law's rough sense
        By equities[4] of self-defence?   80

Di.

Draw the line where you will, it will exclude
Much it should comprehend. I draw it here.

Sp.

        Well, for yourself it may be nice
        To serve vulgarity and vice:
        Must sisters, too, and wives and mothers   85
        Fare like their patient sons and brothers?

Di.

He that loves sister, mother, more than me – [5]

Sp.

        But the injustice – the gross wrong
        To whom on earth does it belong
        If not to you, to whom 'twas done,   90
        Who see it plain as any sun
        To make the base and foul offender
        Confess and satisfaction render?
        At least before the termination of it

4   Equity, according to Aristotle, was the virtue that remedied deficiencies in the
     law.
5   'He that loveth father or mother more than me is not worthy of me: and he that
     loveth son or daughter more than me is not worthy of me' (Mt 10, 37).

> Prove your own lofty reprobation of it.   95
> Though gentleness, I know, was born in you
> Surely you have a little scorn in you?

Di.

Heaven! To pollute one's fingers to pick up
The fallen coin of honour from the dirt!
Pure silver though it be, let it rather lie.   100
To take up any offence, where't may be said
That temper, vanity – I know not what –
Had led me on!
To enter this base crowd and bare one's flanks
To all ill voices of a blustering world;   105
To have so much as e'en half-felt of one
That ever one was angered for oneself!
Beyond suspicion Caesar's wife should be,[6]
Beyond suspicion this bright honour shall.
Did he say scorn? I have some scorn, thank God.   110

Sp.

> Certainly. Only, if it's so
> Let us leave Italy and go
> Post haste, to attend – you're ripe and rank for't
> The Great Peace Meeting up at Frankfort.[7]
> Joy to the Croat! Take our lives,   115
> Sweet friends, and please respect our wives.
> Myself, a trifle quite, you slaughter
> But pray be decent with my daughter.
> Joy to the Croat! Some fine day

---

6   Julius Caesar divorced his wife Pompeia even though her alleged offence was
    quite unproven, on the grounds that he did not wish his wife to be so much as
    suspected.
7   After the German and Austrian revolutions of 1848 a constituent assembly was
    set up in Frankfurt, but by 1850 the revolution had been defeated. The refer-
    ence is probably to a reconstituted diet which in the 1850s tried to keep the
    peace between the different Germanic nations.

He'll see the error of his way,   120
No doubt, and will repent and pray.
At any rate he'll open his eyes
If not before, at the Last Assize.[8]
Not, if I rightly understood you
Not even then, you'd punish, would you?   125
Nay, let the hapless soul escape.
Mere murder, robbery and rape
In whate'er station, age, or sex
Your sacred spirit scarce can vex.
De minimis non curat lex.[9]   130

To the Peace Congress – ring the bell!
Horses to Frankfort and to hell!

Di.
I am not quite in union with myself
On this strange matter. I must needs confess
Instinct turns instinct in and out; and thought   135
Wheels round on thought. To bleed for other's wrongs
In vindication of a Cause, to draw
The sword of the Lord and Gideon[10] – O, that seems
The flower and top of life! But fight because
Some poor misconstruing trifler haps to say   140
I lie, when I do not lie, or is rude
To some vain fashionable thing, some poor
Curl-paper of a doll that's set by chance
To dangle a dull hour on my vext arm,
Why should I? Call you this a Cause? I can't.   145
Oh, he is wrong no doubt. He misbehaves –
But is it worth so much as speaking loud?

8   The Last Judgement.
9   'The law does not trouble itself with trifles'.
10   The most eminent of the judges of Israel, who liberated the Israelites from
     foreign domination.

39

And things more merely personal to myself
Of all earth's things do least affect myself.

Sp.

    Sweet eloquence! At next May Meeting[11]   150
    How it would tell in the repeating!
    I recognise – and kiss the rod –
    The Methodistic voice of God
    I catch contrite that angel whine
    That snuffle human yet divine   155
    The doctrine own, and no mistaker,
    Of the bland Philanthropic Quaker.[12]
    O come, blest age, from bloodshed cease
    Bewildered brothers, dwell at peace.
    This holy effluence from above   160
    Shall fill your wildest hearts with love,
    Shall bring the light of inward day
    To Caffre fierce and sly Malay;[13]
    Soften hard pirates with a kiss
    And melt barbarian isles with bliss –   165
    Leaving, in lieu of war and robbing
    Only a little mild stock-jobbing.

    O doubtless! Let the simple heart
    Mind her own business, do her part,
    Her wrongs repel, maintain her honour   170
    O fiend and savage, out upon her!
    Press, pulpit, from each other borrow
    The terms of scandal, shame, and sorrow;

11 The annual meeting of Evangelical groups of all denominations held at Exeter Hall.
12 William Edward Foster, who in 1850 married Clough's beloved Jane Arnold, was a Quaker philanthropist.
13 Here we see the Victorian stereotypes of the Kaffirs of South Africa and the inhabitants of the regions that are now Malaysia and Indonesia.

Vulgarity shrieks out in fear of it
And piety turns sick to hear of it.   175
The downright things, twixt you and me,
The wrongs we really feel and see
The hurts that actually try one,
Like common plain good deeds close by one,
Decidedly have no existence –   180
They are at such a little distance!
But to protect the lovely figures
Of your half ourang-outang niggers
To preach the doctrine of the cross
To worshippers in house of joss,   185
To take steps for the quick conversion
Of Turk, Armenian, Jew and Persian
Or send up missions, per balloon,
To those poor heathens in the moon –
Oh that – But I'm afraid I storm;   190
I'm quite ashamed to be so warm.

Di.
It may be I am somewhat a poltroon.
I never fought at school. Whether it be
Some native poorness in my spirit's blood,
Or that the holy doctrine of our faith   195
In too exclusive fervency possessed
My heart with feelings, with ideas my brain.

Sp.
Yes; you would argue that it goes
Against the Bible, I suppose
But our revered religion – yes,   200
Our common faith – seems, I confess,
On these points to propose to address
The people more than you or me –
At best the vulgar bourgeoisie.
The sacred writers don't keep count   205

But still the Sermon on the Mount
Must have been spoken, by what's stated,
To hearers by the thousands rated.
Kick a cad's bottom: mild and meek,
He'll turn, we trust, the other cheek.[14]   210
For him it may be right and good;
We are not all of gentle blood
Really, or as such understood.

Di.

There are two kindred upon earth I know –
The oppressors and the oppressed. But as for me,   215
If I must choose to inflict wrong, or accept,
May my last end, and life too, be with these.
Yes, whatso'er the reason – want of blood
Lymphatic humours, or my childhood's faith –
So is the thing, and be it well or ill,   220
I have no choice. I am a man of peace,
And the old Adam of the gentleman
Dares seldom in my bosom stir against
The good plebeian Christian seated there.

Sp.

Forgive me, if I name my doubt,   225
Whether you know '*fort*' means 'get out'.

---

14 In the Sermon on the Mount we are told 'Resist not evil: but whosoever shall smite thee on the right cheek, turn to him the other cheek' (Mt 5, 39).

Scene 6: The Lido

Sp.

What now? the Lido shall it be?
That none may say we didn't see
The ground which Byron used to rise on
And do I don't know what beside on
Ho, *barca*[1] – here and this light gale   5
Will let us run it with a sail.

Di.

I dreamt a dream; till morning light
A bell rang in my head all night
Tinkling and tinkling first, and then
Tolling; and tinkling; tolling again.   10
So brisk and gay, and then so slow.
O joy and terror! mirth and woe!
Ting, ting, there is no God; ting, ting –
Dong, there is no God; dong.
There is no God; dong, dong.   15

Ting, ting, there is no God; ting ting;
Come dance and play, and merrily sing –
Ting, ting a ding, ting, ting a ding.
O pretty girl who trippest along,
Come to my bed – it isn't wrong.   20
Uncork the bottle, sing the song.
Come to my bosom, O my sweet.
For guilt is nonsense, sin deceit
Ere death end us, let us meet.

1 The spirit calls for a boat – something larger than a gondola, needed to cross
the lagoon.

Haven't we trembled long enough   25
Because of that religious stuff?
Come with the witty words and song
And the rich liquor – come along
My charmer – there's no right or wrong.
Ting ting a ting: dong, dong   30
Wine has dregs; the song an end
A silly girl is a poor friend
And age and weakness who shall mend?
Dong, there is no God; dong.

Ting, ting a ding. Come dance and sing!   35
Staid Englishman, who toil and slave
From your first breeching to your grave,
And seldom spend and always save,
And do your duty all your life
By your young family and wife;   40
Come, be't not said you ne'er had known
What earth can furnish you alone.
The Italian, Frenchman, German even,
Have given up all thoughts of heaven;
And you still linger – oh, you fool!   45
Because of what you learnt at school.
You should have gone at least to college,
And got a little ampler knowledge.
Ah well, and yet – dong, dong, dong:
Do as you like, as now you do   50
As work's a cheat, so's pleasure too,
And nothing's new and nothing's true.
Dong, there is no God; dong.

O Rosalie, my precious maid
I think thou thinkest love is true   55
And on thy fragrant bosom laid
I almost could believe it too.
O, in our nook, unknown, unseen,

44

We'll hold our fancy like a screen
Us and the dreadful fact between   60
And it shall yet be long, aye, long
The quiet notes of our low song
Shall keep us from that sad dong, dong.
Hark, hark, hark! O voice of fear:
It reaches us here, even here.   65
Dong, there is no God; dong.

Ring ding, ring ding, tara tara,
To battle, to battle, haste, haste
To battle, to battle, aha, aha
On, on to the conqueror's feast!   70
From west and east and south and north
Ye men of valour and of worth
Ye mighty men of arms – come forth
And work your will, for that is just
And in your impulse put your trust,   75
Beneath your feet the fools are dust.
Alas, alas! O grief and wrong
The good are weak, the wicked strong;
And O my God, how long how long?
Dong, there is no God; dong.   80

Ring ting; to bow before the strong
There is a rapture too in this;
Speak, outraged maiden, in thy wrong
Did terror bring no secret bliss?
Were boys' shy lips worth half a song   85
Compared to the hot soldier's kiss?
Work for thy master, work thou slave,
He is not merciful, but brave.
Be't joy to serve, who free and proud
Scorns thee and all the ignoble crowd;   90
Take that, 'tis all thou art allowed,
Except the snaky hope that they

My some time serve, who rule to-day
When, by hell-demons, shan't they pay?
O wickedness, O shame and grief,   95
And heavy load, and no relief!
O God, O God! and which is worst,
To be the curser or the curst,
The victim or the murderer? Dong
Dong, there is no God; dong.   100

Ring ding, ring ding, tara tara,
Away, and hush that preaching – fagh!
Ye vulgar dreamers about peace,
Who offer noblest hearts, to heal
The tenderest hurts honour can feel   105
Paid magistrates and the Police!
O piddling merchant justice, go,
Exacter rules than yours we know;
Resentment's rule, and that high law
Of whoso best the sword can draw.   110
Ah well, and yet, dong, dong, dong.
Go on my friends, as now you do;
Lawyers are villains, soldiers too;
And nothing's new and nothing's true,
Dong, there is no God; dong.   115

O Rosalie, my lovely maid
I think thou thinkest love is true
And on thy faithful bosom laid
I almost could believe it too.
The villainies, the wrongs, the alarms   120
Forget we in each other's arms.
No justice here, no God above
But where we are, is there not love?
What? what? thou also go'st? For how
Should dead truth live in lover's vow?   125
What, thou? thou also lost? Dong
Dong, there is no God; dong.

I had a dream, from eve to light
A bell went sounding all the night.
Gay mirth, black woe; thin joys, huge pain: 130
I tried to stop it, but in vain.
It ran right on, and never broke;
Only when day began to stream
Through the white curtains to my bed,
And like an angel at my head   135
Light stood and touched me – I awoke
And looked, and said, 'It is a dream'.

Sp.

Not so bad, neither, by my fay
A pretty price for a fine day;
You've read your Béranger I see   140
– Voltaire perhaps? – and thought of me.
But really you own some apology
For harping thus upon theology.
I'm not a judge, I own, in short
Religion may not be my forte.   145
The Church of England I belong to,
But think Dissenters not far wrong too;
They're vulgar dogs, but for his *creed*
I hold that no man will be d—d.
My Establishment I much respect   150
Her ordinances don't neglect;
Attend at Church on Sunday once
And in the Prayer-book am no dunce;
Baptise my babies; nay my wife
Would be churched[2] too once in her life 155
She's taken, I regret to state
Rather a Puseyite[3] turn of late.

2   Churching was a ceremony of purification of women after childbirth, practised
    by High Church Anglicans and Roman Catholics.
3   After the conversion of John Henry Newman to Catholicism, the undoubted
    leader of the High Church faction was Edward Bouverie Pusey.

To set the thing quite right, I went
At Easter to the Sacrament.
'Tis proper, once a year or so   160
To do the civil thing and show –
But come and listen in your turn
And you shall hear and mark and learn.

'There is no God' the wicked saith
           'And truly it's a blessing   165
For what he might have done with us
           It's better only guessing.'

'There is no God' a youngster thinks
           'Or really if there may be
He surely didn't mean a man   170
           Always to be a baby.'

'There is no God, or if there is'
           The tradesman thinks, ''twere funny
If he should take it ill in me
           To make a little money.'   175

'Whether there be,' the rich man says
           'It matters very little,
For I and mine, thank somebody,
           Are not in want of victual.'

Some others, also, to themselves   180
           Who scarce so much as doubt it,
Think there is none, when they are well,
           And do not think about it.

But country folks who live beneath
           The shadow of the steeple;   185
The parson and the parson's wife,
           And mostly married people;

Youths green and happy in first love,
    So thankful for illusion;
And men caught out in what the world   190
    Calls guilt, in first confusion;

And almost every one when age,
    Disease, or sorrows strike him,
Inclines to think there is a God
    Or something very like Him.   195

    But *eccoci!* with our *barchetta*
    Here at the Sant' Elisabetta.[4]

Di.
Vineyards and maize, that's pleasant for sore eyes.

Sp.

    And on the island's other side
    The place where Murray's faithful guide[5]   200
    Informs us Byron used to ride.

Di.
These trellised vines! enchanting! Sandhills, ho!
The sea, at last, the sea – the real broad sea –
Beautiful! and a glorious breeze upon it.

Sp.

    Look back; one catches at this station   205
    Lagoon and sea in combination.

Di.

    On her still lake the city sits,
    Where bark and boat about her flits

4   The boat has now reached the jetty of Santa Maria Elisabetta, the main arrival
    point of the Lido.
5   Murray's volumes were the indispensable companion of the Victorian trav-
    eller in Italy.

Nor dreams, her soft siesta taking,
Of Adriatic billows breaking.   210
I do, and see and hear them. Come! To the sea!

Sp.

The wind I think is the *sirocco*[6]
Yonder, I take it, is Malmocco.[7]
Thank you! It never was my passion
To skip o'er sandhills in that fashion.   215

Di.

Oh a grand surge! We'll bathe; quick, quick! undress!
Quick, quick! In, in!
We'll take the crested billows by their backs
And shake them. Quick! in, in!
And I will taste again the old joy   220
I gloried in so when a boy.

Sp.

Well; but it's not so pleasant for the feet;
We should have brought some towels and a sheet.

Di.

In, in! I go. Ye great winds blow
And break, thou curly wave, upon my breast.   225

Sp.

H'm. I'm undressing. Doubtless all is well.
I only wish these thistles were at hell.
By heaven, I'll stop before that bad yet worse is,
And take care of our watches – and our purses.

---

6 The hot, oppressive, southern wind.
7 The village of Malamocco, near the east end of the island, is one of the few
   places that has preserved the rural Victorian aspect of the Lido.

Di.
Aha! come, come, great waters, roll!   230
Accept me, take me, body and soul!
Aha!

Sp.

     Come, no more of that stuff,
     I'm sure you've stayed in long enough.

Di.

     That's done me good. It grieves me though
     I never came here long ago.   235

Sp.

     Pleasant perhaps. However, no offence
     Animal spirits are not common sense.
     You think perhaps I have outworn them;
     They're good enough as an assistance
     But in themselves a poor existence.   240
     But you – with this one bathe, no doubt,
     Have solved all questions out and out.
     'Tis Easter Day, and on the Lido
     Lo, Christ the Lord is risen indeed, O!

Entr'acte: In a Gondola

Di.

Per ora.[1] To the Grand Canal
Afterwards e'en as fancy shall.

Afloat we move. Delicious! Ah,
What else is like the gondola?
This level floor of liquid glass   5
Begins beneath it swift to pass.
It goes as though it went alone
By some impulsion of its own.
How light it moves, how softly! Ah,
Were all things like the gondola!   10

How light it moves, how softly! Ah,
Could life, as does our gondola,
Unvexed with quarrels, aims, and cares,
And moral duties and affairs,
Unswaying, noiseless, swift, and strong,   15
For ever thus, thus glide along!
How light we move, how softly! Ah,
Were all things like the gondola!

With no more motion than should bear
A freshness to the languid air;   20
With no more effort than exprest
The need and naturalness of rest,
Which we beneath a grateful shade
Should take on peaceful pillows laid –

1   'By the hour'. Dipsychus is making his contract with the gondolier.

How light we move, how softly, Ah   25
Were all things like the gondola.

In one unbroken passage borne
To closing night from opening morn,
Uplift at while slow eyes to mark
Some palace front, some passing bark;   30
Through windows catch the varying shore,
And hear the soft turns of the oar –
How light we move, how softly! Ah,
Were all things like the gondola!

So live, nor need to call to mind!   35
Our slaving brother set behind!

Sp.

Pooh! Nature meant him for no better
Than our most humble menial debtor
Who thanks us for his day's employment
As we our purse for our enjoyment.   40

Di.

To make one's fellow man an instrument – [2]

Sp.

Is just the thing that makes him most content.

Di.

Our gaieties, our luxuries
          Our pleasures and our glee
Mere insolence and wantonries   45
          Alas! they feel to me.

---

2   It was a maxim of Kant's moral philosophy that one should 'always treat
humanity, whether in your own person or in the person of any other, never
simply as a means'.

How shall I laugh and sing and dance?
    My very heart recoils,
While here to give my mirth a chance
    A hungry brother toils.   50

The joy that does not spring from joy
    Which I in others see
Now can I venture to employ,
    Or find it joy for me?[3]

Sp.

Oh, come, come, come! By Him that set us here, 55
Who's to enjoy at all, pray let us hear?
You won't, he can't! Oh, no more fuss!
What's it to him, or he to us?
Sing, sing away, be glad and gay
And don't forget that we shall pay   60
How light we move, how softly! Ah,
Tra lal la la, the gondola

Di.
Yes, it is beautiful ever, let foolish men rail at it never.
Yes, it is beautiful truly, my brothers, I grant it you duly
Wise are ye others that choose it, and happy ye all that can
    use it.   65
Life is beautiful wholly, and could we eliminate only
This interfering, enslaving, o'ermastering demon of craving,
This wicked temper inside us to ruin still eager to guide us
Life were beatitude, action a possible pure satisfaction.

Ah, but it will not, it may not, its nature and law is to stay not 70
This semi-vision enchanting with but actuality wanting,
And as a picture or book at, this life that is lovely to look at

---

3   These verses, like many others in this entr'acte, seem originally to have been
    self-standing poems written by Clough as independent pieces, or in different
    contexts, and only later inserted in *Dipsychus*.

When that it comes as we go on to th'eating and drinking
    and so on
Is not beatitude, Action in no way pure satisfaction.[4]

Sp.

             (Hexameters, by all that's odious   75
             Beshod with rhyme to run melodious)

Di.

All as I go on my way I behold them consorting and coupling;
Faithful, it seemeth, and fond; very fond, very possibly faithful;
All as I go on my way with a pleasure sincere and unmingled.
Life it is beautiful truly, my brothers, I grant it you duly;   80
But for perfection attaining is one method only, abstaining;
Let us abstain, for we should do, if only we thought that we
    could so.

Sp.

             Ancora! bravo! but this time
             I think you have forgot your rhyme
             Not that on that account your verse   85
             Could be much better or much worse
             To make it's doubtless very pleasant
             But to hear – *basta* – for the present.

             This world is very odd, we see
                  We little comprehend it   90
             But in one fact can all agree
                  God won't, and we can't, mend it.

             Being common sense, it can't be sin
                  To take it as we find it;
             The pleasure to take pleasure in;   95
                  The pain, try not to mind it.

---

4   These stanzas, and Dipsychus's next speech, in hexameters as the Spirit
    remarks, are expansions of a passage in Clough's *Amours de Voyage*, III, viii.

Dipsychus

Di.
Better it were, thou sayest, to consent
Feast while we may, and live ere life be spent;
Close up clear eyes, and call the unstable sure,
The unlovely lovely and the filthy pure   100
In self-belyings, self-deceivings roll
And lose in Action, Passion, Talk, the soul.

Nay, better far to mark off thus much air
And call it heaven, place bliss and glory there;
Fix perfect homes in the unsubstantial sky   105
And say, what is not, will be by-and-by;
What here exists not, must exist elsewhere.
But play no tricks upon thy soul, O man;
Let fact be fact, and life the thing it can.

Sp.
    To these remarks so sage and clerkly   110
        Worthy of Malebranche or Berkeley[5]
    I trust it won't be deemed a sin
        If I too answer 'with a grin'

    These juicy meats, this flashing wine,
        May be an unreal mere appearance   115
    Only, for my inside in fine
        They show a singular coherence

    This lovely creature's glowing charms
        Are gross illusion, I don't doubt that
    But folded in each other's arms   120
        We somehow didn't think about that:

5 The French philosopher Malebranche and the Irish Bishop Berkeley both maintained the theory that sensory appearance was a direct creation of God rather than an experience of a material world.

Dipsychus

Oh yes, my pensive youth, abstain:
    And any empty sick sensation
Any fierce hunger, any pain
    You'll know is mere imagination.   125

Trust me, I've read your German sage[6]
    To far more purpose e'er than you did
You find it in his wisest page
    Whom God deludes is well deluded.

San Giorgio and the Redentore![7]   130
This Gothic is a worn-out story
No building, trivial, gay, or solemn
Can spare the shapely Grecian column.
'Tis not, these centuries four, for nought
Our European world of thought   135
Has made familiar to its home
The classic mind of Greece and Rome;
In all new work that would look forth
To more than antiquarian worth,
Palladio's pediments and bases,   140
Or something such, will find their places.
Maturer optics[8] don't delight
In childish dim religious light,
In evanescent vague effects
That shirk, not face, one's intellects;   145
They love not fancies fast betrayed,
And artful tricks of light and shade,
But pure form nakedly displayed,
And all things absolutely made.

---

6   Goethe, who in his rhymed distichs wrote 'Wen Gott betrügt, ist wohl betrogen'.
7   Two of the finest Palladian churches in Venice, disparaged in Ruskin's *Seven Lamps of Architecture* in comparison with the Gothic masterpiece of the Doge's palace (see line 151 below).
8   Pretentious slang for 'eyes', typical of the Spirit's style (cf. 'pelf', 'cad' below).

The Doge's palace, though, from hence,⠀⠀⠀⠀150
In spite of Ruskin's d—d pretence,
The tide now level with the quay,
Is certainly a thing to see.[9]
We'll turn to the Rialto soon;
One's told to see it by the moon.⠀⠀⠀⠀155

A gondola here, and a gondola there,
'Tis the pleasantest fashion of taking the air
To right and to left; stop, turn, and go yonder,
And let us repeat, o'er the flood as we wander
⠀⠀⠀How pleasant it is to have money, heigh ho⠀⠀160
⠀⠀⠀How pleasant it is to have money.

As I sat at the café I said to myself
They may talk as they please about what they call pelf,
They may sneer as they like about eating and drinking
But help it I cannot, I cannot help thinking⠀⠀⠀⠀165
⠀⠀⠀How pleasant it is to have money, heigh ho
⠀⠀⠀How pleasant it is to have money.

Come along, 'tis the time, ten or more minutes past
And he who came first had to wait for the last;
The oysters ere this had been in and been out;⠀⠀170
While I have been sitting and thinking about
⠀⠀⠀How pleasant it is to have money, heigh ho
⠀⠀⠀How pleasant it is to have money.

A clear soup with eggs; *voilà tout*; of the fish
The *filets de sole* are a moderate dish⠀⠀⠀⠀175
A la Orly, but you're for red mullet you say;
By the gods of good fare, who can question today

9⠀⠀The Spirit agrees that the Doge's palace, even though wildly overvalued by
⠀⠀Ruskin, is well worth seeing.

How pleasant it is to have money, heigh ho
How pleasant it is to have money.

After oysters, sauterne; then sherry; champagne,   180
Ere one bottle goes, comes another again;
Fly up, thou bold cork, to the ceiling above
And tell to our ears in the sound that they love
How pleasant it is to have money, heigh ho
How pleasant it is to have money.   185

I've the simplest of palates; absurd it may be
But I almost could dine on a *poulet-au-riz,*
Fish and soup and omelette and that – but the deuce
There were to be woodcocks, and not *Charlotte Russe*
So pleasant it is to have money, heigh ho   190
So pleasant it is to have money.

Your chablis is acid, away with the hock,
Give me the pure juice of the purple Médoc:
St Peray is exquisite ; but, if you please,
Some Burgundy just before tasting the cheese   195
So pleasant it is to have money, heigh ho
So pleasant it is to have money.

As for that, pass the bottle, and d—n the expense,
I've seen it observed by a writer of sense,
That the labouring classes could scarce live a day,   200
If people like us didn't eat, drink, and pay.
So useful it is to have money, heigh ho
So useful it is to have money.

I sit at my table *en grand seigneur*
And when I have done, throw a crust to the poor;   205
Not only the pleasure itself of good living,
But also the pleasure of now and then giving.
So pleasant it is to have money, heigh-ho
So pleasant it is to have money.

I drive through the streets and I care not a d—n   210
The people look up and they ask who I am;
And if I should chance to run over a cad
I can pay for the damage, if ever so bad.
      So useful it is to have money, heigh ho
      So useful it is to have money.   215

We stroll to our box, and look down on the pit
If it weren't rather low should be tempted to spit.
We loll and we talk until people look up
And when it's half over we go out and sup
      So pleasant it is to have money, heigh ho   220
      So pleasant it is to have money.

The best of the rooms and the best of the fare
And as for all others the devil may care
It isn't our fault, if they dare not afford
To sup like a prince and be drunk as a lord.   225
      So pleasant it is to have money, heigh ho
      So pleasant it is to have money.

A gondola here and a gondola there
'Tis the pleasantest fashion of taking the air
To right and to left; stop, turn and go yonder   230
And let us repeat o'er the tide as we wander
      How pleasant it is to have money, heigh ho,
      How pleasant it is to have money.

Di.
      How light we go, how soft we skim
      And all in moonlight seem to swim!   235
      The south side rises o'er our bark,
      A wall impenetrably dark;
      The north the while profusely bright
      The water – is it shade or light?
      Say, gentle moon, which conquers now   240

The flood, those massy hulls,[10] or thou?
How light we go, how softly, Ah!
Were life but as the gondola!

How light we go, how soft we skim,
And all in moonlight seem to swim!   245
In moonlight is it now – or shade?
In planes of sure division made
By angles sharp of palace walls
The clear light and the shadow falls
O sight of glory, sight of wonder!   250
Seen, a pictorial portent under
O great Rialto, the vast round
Of thy thrice-solid arch profound.
How light we go, how softly! Ah,
Life should be as the gondola!   255
How light we go, how softly –

Sp.

             Nay
'Fore heaven, enough of that today;
I'm deadly weary of your tune,
And half *ennuyé* with the moon;
The shadows lie, the glories fall,   260
And are but moonshine after all.
It goes against my conscience really
To let myself feel so ideally.
Make me repose no power of man shall
In things so deuced unsubstantial.   265
Come, for the Piazzetta steer;
'Tis nine o'clock or very near.

10 At this point the gondola appears to be at the north-western end of the island,
where, then as now, large sea-going vessels berthed. In the next stanza the pair
retrace their route back down the Grand Canal, under the Rialto bridge, ending
up at the Piazzetta, between St Mark's and the Lagoon.

These airy blisses, skiey joys
Of vague romantic girls and boys
Which melt the heart (and the brain soften)   270
When not affected, as too often
They are, remind me, I protest
Of nothing better at the best
Than Timon's feast to his ancient lovers,
Warm water under silver covers;   275
'Lap, dogs!' I think I hear him say
And lap who will, so I'm away.[11]

Di.

How light we go, how soft we skim,
And all in open moonlight swim!
Bright clouds against, reclined I mark   280
The white dome now projected dark
And, by o'er-brilliant lamps displayed
The Doge's columns and arcade;
Over still waters mildly come
The distant laughter and the hum.   285
How light we go, how softly! Ah,
Life should be as the gondola!

Sp.

The Devil! We've had enough of you
Quote us a little Wordsworth, do!
Those lines that are so just, they say: 290
'A something far more deeply' – eh?
Interfused – what is it they tell us?
Which and the sunset are bedfellows.[12]

---

11 Timon of Athens, in Shakespeare's play of that name, invites his false friends
   to a banquet at which the covered dishes contain only warm water, and then
   invites them to partake with the words 'Uncover, dogs, and lap' (III, vi, 82).
12 Wordsworth's *Lines above Tintern Abbey* speak of 'a sense sublime / Of some-
   thing far more deeply interfused / whose dwelling is the light of setting suns'.

Di.

    How light we go, how soft we skim
    And all in open moonlight swim!   295
    Ah, gondolier, slow, slow more slow!
    We go; but wherefore thus should go?
    Ah, let not muscle all too strong
    Beguile, betray thee to our wrong!
    On to the landing, onward. Nay,   300
    Sweet dream, a little longer stay!
    On to the landing; here. And ah,
    Life is not as the gondola!

Sp.

    Tre ore. So. The Parthenone
    Is it, you haunt for your *limone*?   305
    Let me induce you now to join me
    In *gramolata persici.*[13]

13 Paying off the gondoliers, the Spirit observes that he owes them for three hours. He then invites Dipsychus to join him, in a café named after the Parthenon, in an iced drink of crushed peaches.

ACT II

Scene 1: The Academy[1]

Di.

A modern daub it was perchance;
I know not; but I dare be sure
From Titian's hues no connoisseur
Had turned one condescending glance

Where Byron, somewhat drest up, draws   5
His sword, impatient long, and speaks
Unto a tribe of motley Greeks
His pledge word unto their brave cause.[2]

Not far, assumed to mystic bliss
Behold the ecstatic Virgin rise!   10
Ah, wherefore vainly, to fond eyes
That melt in burning tears for this?

Yet if we *must* live, as would seen
These peremptory heats to claim,
Ah, not for profit, not for fame,   15
And not for pleasure's giddy dream,

And not for piping empty reeds,
And not for colouring idle dust

1 The Accademia di Belle Arti, home of Titian's renowned *Assumption of the Virgin*.
2 In 1823 Lord Byron joined the Greek insurgents who were rebelling against Turkish rule, and died the next year of fever at Missolonghi. The painter of 'the modern daub' has not been identified.

If live we positively must
God's name be blest for noble deeds.[3]   20

Verses! well, they are made, so let them go;
No more if I can help. This is one way
The procreant heat and fervour of our youth
Escapes, in puff, and smoke, and shapeless words
Of mere ejaculation, nothing worth,   25
Unless to make maturer years content
To slave in base compliance to the world.

What wilt thou be, my soul?
                              The Student?
Musty as his books and dingier than their backs
Convinced that life of life is their dead words   30
Than which himself is deader? The tutor?
Whoring his sweet experience? Nay; the Fop
Making the universe his looking glass
To tell him falsehoods. The man of the world?
Hardening his heart and suppling still his back   35
Most proud when on others preying, and
Than all those others most himself a prey.
                    Say, then, the Pietist?
Lifting his prayerful eyeballs to his Heaven
While with his nether part (as needs must be)   40
He plays the trick of the harlot. Shall we say
The Politician, all a got-up cry,
Merchant, all costing, lawyer, all lies hid
The wit, all spangle, gentleman, all gloss
Tradesman, all meek, philosopher all fool.   45
Which of all these will thou become, my soul
Which of them all; thou mayest be any one,
Thou canst be any, and shouldst not be none.

---

3   The message, less than transparently expressed, is that life should be lived not
    for profit, fame, pleasure, poetry, or painting, but for the sake of noble deeds
    (such as Byron's commitment to the Greek cause).

Which of all these wilt thou become, my soul?
                    The Man of Action   50
Losing his impulse in a shoal of minnows
Still flocking into sand –
                    The Man of Thought
· Bartering his honesty for time to think
Those thoughts which then desert him
                    of Religion   55
Tied to a vision and debasing that
With false and foolish service
                    or he of Virtue
Fanaticising good –
                    The man of Pleasure then
Killing it, and leaving his quick age, disease,
Foul thoughts, and void –   60
                    Or the man of Sense
That is to say, one of the vulgar herd
Tethered to feed, and mating as they meet
Feeding and breeding, littering where they lie
O'er peopling earth with half the race
Who making no election leave it all   65
To God or Chance, it doesn't matter which.
What of all those wilt thou become, my Soul?

I have scarce spoken yet to this strange follower
Whom I picked up – ye great gods, tell me where!
And when! for I remember such long years   70
And yet he seems new come. I commune with myself;
He speaks, I hear him, and resume myself;
Whate'er I think he adds his comments to;
Which yet not interrupts me. Scarce I know
If ever once directly I addressed him.   75
Let me essay it now, for I have strength.
Yet, what he wants, and what he fain would have,
O, I know all too surely; not in vain,
Although unnoticed has he dogged my ear.

Come, we'll be definite, explicit, plain;   80
I can resist, I know; and 'twill be well
To have used for colloquy this manlier mood,
Which is to last, ye chances, say, how long?
How shall I call him? Mephistopheles?

Sp.
I come, I come.

Di.
          So quick, so eager; ha!   85
Like an eaves-dropping menial on my thought,
With something of an exultation too, methinks,
Out-peeping in that springy jaunty gait.
I doubt about it. Shall I do it? Oh! Oh!
Shame on me! Come! Should I, my follower   90
Should I conceive (not that at all I do)
'Tis curiosity that prompts my speech) –
But should I form, a thing to be supposed
A wish to bargain for your merchandise,
Say what were your demands? What were your terms?   95
What should I do, what should I cease to do?
What incense on what altars should I burn?
And what abandon? what unlearn or learn?
Religion goes, I take it.

Sp.
          Oh
You'll go to church of course, you know   100
Or at the least will take a pew
To send your wife and servants to.
Trust me, I make a point of that;
No infidelity, that's flat.

Di.

Religion is not in a pew, say some   105
Cucullus *you* hold, *facit* monachum.[4]

Sp.

        Why, as to feelings of devotion
        I interdict all vague emotion;
        But if you will, for once and all,
        Compound with ancient Juvenal[5]   110
        Orandum est, one perfect prayer
        For savoir-vivre, savoir-faire.

        Theology – don't recommend you
        Unless, turned lawyer, Heaven should send you
        In your profession's way a case   115
        Of Baptism and Prevenient Grace;[6]
        But that's not likely. I'm inclined
        All circumstances borne in mind,
        To think (to keep you in due borders)
        You'd better enter holy orders.   120

Di.
On that, my friend, you'd better not insist.

Sp.

        Well, well, 'tis but a good thing missed.
        The item's optional no doubt;
        But how to get you bread without?

4   Dipsychus reverses the proverb 'Cucullus non facit monachum' = 'it is not the
    cowl that makes the monk'.
5   The Roman satirist Juvenal wrote 'orandum est ut sit mens sana in corpore
    sano' = 'you must pray for a sound mind in a sound body'.
6   In March 1850 the Privy Council determined an ecclesiastical case in favour of
    a Low Church clergyman, C. Gorham, who had been refused installation in his
    parish by a High Church bishop on the grounds that he did not believe that
    grace was conferred at the moment of the act of baptism.

You'll marry; I shall find the lady.   125
Make your proposal and be steady.

Di.

Marry, ill spirit! and at your sole choice?
De Rigeur! Can't give you a voice.

Sp.

What matter! Oh, trust one who knows you
You'll make an admirable *sposo*.[7]   130
Una bella donn' un' gran' riposo[8]
As said the soldier in our carriage
Although he didn't mean in marriage.
As to the rest I shall not quarrel,
You being, as it seems, *so* moral.   135
Though, orders laid upon the shelf
In merest justice to myself
But that I hate the pro and con of it
I should have made a *sine-qua-non* of it.
Come, my dear boy, I will not bind you,   140
But scruples must be cast behind you.
All mawkish talking I dislike
But when the iron *is* hot, strike
Good God! to think of youthful bliss
Restricted to a sneaking kiss.   145

Di.
Enough. But action – look to that well, mind me;
See that some not unworthy work you find me;
If man I be, then give the man expression.

Sp.

Of course you'll enter a profession;
If not the Church, why then the Law.   150

7   Husband.
8   'A beautiful woman is a great comfort'.

69

By Jove, we'll teach you how to draw!⁹
Once in the way that you should go
You'll do your business well, I know
Besides, the best of the concern is
I'm hand in glove with the attorneys.   155
With them and me to help, don't doubt
But in due season you'll come out;
Leave Kelly, Cockburn in the lurch.¹⁰
And yet, do think about the Church.
By all that's rich, 'twould do me good   160
To fig you out in robe and hood.
Wouldn't I give up wine and wench
To mount you fairly on the bench.

Di.
'Tis well, ill spirit, I admire your wit;
As for your wisdom, I shall think of it.   165
And now farewell.

9   To prepare a legal document.
10 Sir Fitzroy Kelly was Solicitor General in 1845–46, and Sir Alexander Cockburn
     (later Lord Chief Justice) in 1850.

Scene 2

Di.
The Law! 'twere honester, if 'twere genteel,
To say the dung-cart. What! shall I go about
And like the walking shoeblack roam the flags[1]
With heedful eyes, down bent, and like a glass
In a sea-captain's hand sweeping all round,   5
To see whose boots are dirtiest? Oh the luck
To stoop and clean a pair!

Religion: – if indeed it be in vain
To expect to find in this more modern time
That which the old world styled, in old-world phrase   10
Walking with God, it seems his newer will
We should not think of him at all, but trudge it
And of the world he has assigned us make
What best we can.

        Then love: I scarce can think
That these be-maddening discords of the mind   15
To pure melodious sequence could be changed,
And all the vext conundrums of our life
Prove to all time bucolically solved
By a new Adam and a second Eve
Set in a garden which no serpent seeks   20
And yet I hold heart can beat true to heart:
And to hew down the tree which bears this fruit,
To do a thing which cuts me off from hope,
To falsify the movement of love's mind,
To seat some alien trifler on the throne   25

1   Paving stones.

A queen may come to claim – that were ill done.
What! to the close hand of the clutching Jew
Hand up that rich reversion! and for what?
This would be hard, did I indeed believe
'Twould ever fall. But love, the large repose   30
Restorative, not to mere outside needs
Skin-deep, but thoroughly to the total man,
Exists, I will believe, but so, so rare,
So doubtful, so exceptional, hard to guess;
When guessed, so often counterfeit; in brief,   35
A thing not possibly to be conceived
An item in the reckonings of the wise.

Action, that staggers me. For I had hoped,
'Midst weakness, indolence, frivolity,
Irresolution, still had hoped, and this   40
Seems sacrificing hope. Better to wait:
The wise men wait; it is the foolish haste,
And ere the scenes are in their slides[2] would play,
And while the instruments are tuning, dance.
I see Napoleon on the heights, intent   45
To arrest that one brief unit of loose time
Which hands high Victory's thread; his Marshals fret,
His soldiers clamour low: the very guns
Seem going off of themselves; the cannon strain
Like hell-dogs in the leash. But he, he waits;   50
And lesser chances and inferior hopes
Meantime go pouring past. Men gnash their teeth;
The very faithful have begun to doubt;
But they molest not the calm eye that seeks
'Midst all this huddling silver little worth   55
The one thin piece that comes, pure gold. He waits.
Oh me, when the great deed e'en now has broke

2   Runners for scenery.

Like a man's hand the horizon's level line,[3]
So soon to fill the zenith with rich clouds;
Oh, in this narrow interspace, this moment,   60
This list and selvage[4] of a glorious time
To despair of the great and sell to the mean!
Oh, thou of little faith, what hast thou done?[5]

Yet if the occasion coming should find *us*
Undexterous, incapable? In light things   65
Prove thou the arms thou long'st to glorify
Nor fear to work up from the lowest ranks
Whence come great Nature's captains. And high deeds
Haunt not the fringy edges of the fight,
But the pell-mell of men. Of, what and if   70
E'en now by lingering here I let them slip
Like an unpractised spyer through a glass
Still pointing to the blank; too high. And yet
In dead details to smother vital ends
Which should give life to them; in the deft trick   75
Of prentice-handling to forget great art,
To base mechanical adroitness yield
The Inspiration and the Hope, a slave!
Oh, and to blast that Innocence, which, though
Here it may seem a dull unopening bud,   80
May yet bloom freely in celestial clime.

Were it not better done, then, to keep off
And see, not share, the strife; stand out the waltz

---

3   1 Kings 18, 21: 'There ariseth a little cloud out of the sea, like a man's hand' –
    presaging the end of a great drought.
4   'List' and 'selvage' are both words for the edge of a piece of fabric.
5   'O ye of little faith' is a phrase often on the lips of Jesus (e.g. Mt 6, 30). The point
    of the quotation here is that Dipsychus is adjuring himself not to engage prema-
    turely in some project of action: he should have faith that some great venture
    is in store for him in the future, and wait patiently, like Napoleon, for it to
    present itself.

Which fools whirl dizzy in? Is it possible?
Contamination taints the idler first.   85
And without base compliance e'en that same
Which buys bold hearts free course, Earth lends not these
Their pent and miserable standing room.
Life loves no lookers-on at his great game
And with boy's malice still delights to turn   90
The tide of sport upon the sitters-by
And set observers scampering with their notes.
'Tis but in petty battles men submit
Their acts to registration. In great fights
Our correspondent of the morning news   95
Were brushed away as an impertinence.
Oh, it is great to do and know not what,
Nor let it e'er be known. The dashing stream
Strays not to pick his steps among the rocks,
Or let his water-breaks be chronicled.   100
And though the hunter looks before he leap,
'Tis instinct rather than a shaped-out thought
That lifts him his bold way. Then, instinct, hail,
And farewell hesitation! If I stay,
I am not innocent; nor if I go –   105
E'en should I fail – beyond redemption lost.

Ah, if I had a course like a full stream
If life were as the field of chase! No, no;
The age of instinct has, it seems, gone by,
And will not be forced back. And to live now   110
I must sluice out myself into canals
And lose all force in ducts. The modern Hotspur
Shrills not his trumpet of 'To Horse, to Horse!'[6]

---

6 In Shakespeare's *Henry IV, Part 1* Harry Hotspur, in rebellion against the King
   and his son Harry, says 'come, let me taste my horse / who is to bear me like
   a thunderbolt / against the bosom of the Prince of Wales. / Harry to Harry shall,
   hot horse to horse / meet and ne'er part till one drop down a corse'.

But consults columns in a railway guide;
A demigod of figures, an Achilles[7]   115
Of computation,
A verier Mercury,[8] express come down
To *do* the world with swift arithmetic.
Well, one could bear with that; were the end ours,
One's choice and the correlative of the soul   120
To drudge were then sweet service. But indeed
The earth moves slowly, if it move at all,
And by the general, not the single force
Of the link'd members of the vast machine,
In all those crowded rooms of industry   125
No individual soul has loftier leave
Than fiddling with a piston or a valve.
Well, one could bear that also: one could drudge
And do one's petty part, and be content
In base manipulation, solaced still   130
By thinking of the leagued fraternity,
And of co-operation and the effect
Of the great engine. If indeed it work
And is not a mere treadmill! Which it may be;
Who can confirm it is not? We ask Action,   135
And dream of arms and conflict; and string up
All self-devotion's muscles; and are set
To fold up papers.[9] To what end? We know not.
Other folks do so; it is always done;
And it perhaps is right. And we are paid for it   140
For nothing else we can be. He that eats
Must serve, and serve as other servants do:
And don the lacquey's livery of the house.
Oh, could I shoot my thought up to the sky,

7   The Greek paladin of Homer's *Iliad*.
8   In Roman mythology, the messenger of the gods.
9   Eerily predictive of Clough's later service to Florence Nightingale, as maliciously summed up by Lytton Strachey: 'parcels to be done up in brown paper, and carried to the post'.

A column of pure shape, for all to observe!   145
But I must slave, a meagre coral-worm
To build beneath the tide with excrement
What one day will be island, or be reef,
And will feed men, or wreck them. Well, well, well.
Adieu ye twisted thinkings. I submit.   150

Action is what one must get, it is clear
And one could dream it better than one finds,
In its kind personal, in its motive not;
Not selfish as it now is, nor as now
Maiming the individual. If we had that,   155
It would cure all indeed. Oh how would then
These pitiful rebellions of the flesh
These caterwaulings of the effeminate heart,
These hurts of self-imagined dignity,
Pass like the seaweed from about the bows   160
Of a great vessel speeding straight to sea!
Yes, if we could have that; but I suppose
We shall not have it, and therefore I submit.

Sp. (from within)

        Submit, submit!
        'Tis common sense, and human wit   165
        Can claim no higher name than it
        Submit, submit!

        Devotion, and ideas, and love
        And beauty claim their place above;
        But saint and sage and poet's dreams   170
        Divide the light in coloured streams,
        Which this alone gives all combined
        The *siccum lumen*[10] of the mind

10 'Dry light' – an expression used by philosophers, from Heraclitus to Spinoza,
    to refer to completely disinterested intellectual activity.

Called common sense: and no high wit
Gives better counsel than does it.   175
Submit, submit!

To see things simply as they are
Here, at our elbows, transcends far
Trying to spy out some new star
Which may or may not be; and if known   180
Improves the stellar chart alone.
No philosophic gift outweighs
The plain good common sense that says
Submit, submit!

'Tis common sense, and human wit   185
Can ask no higher name than it.
Submit! Submit!

O did you think you were alone?
That I was so unfeeling grown
As not with joy to leave behind   190
My ninety-nine in hope to find
(How sweet the words my sense express!)
My lost sheep in the wilderness?[11]

---

11 Luke 15, 4: 'What man of you, having an hundred sheep, if he lose one of them,
    doth not leave the ninety and nine in the wilderness, and go after that which
    is lost, until he find it?'

Scene 3: The Piazza, at night

Di.
There have been times, not many, but enough
To quiet all repinings of the heart;
There have been times, in which my tranquil soul,
No longer nebulous, sparse, errant, seemed
Upon its axis solidly to move,   5
Centred and fast; no mere chaotic blank
For random rays to traverse unretained,
But rounding luminous its fair ellipse
Around its central sun.
                  O happy hours!
O compensation ample for long days   10
Of what impatient tongues call wretchedness!
O beautiful, beneath the magic moon
To walk the watery way of palaces!
O beautiful, o'er vaulted with gemmed blue,
This spacious court;[1] with colour and with gold   15
With cupolas, and pinnacles, and points,
And crosses multiplex, and tips and balls
(Wherewith the bright stars unreproving mix
Nor scorn by hasty eyes to be confused).
Fantastically perfect this low pile   20
Of oriental glory; these long ranges
Of classic chiselling, this gay flickering crowd
And the calm Campanile.[2] Beautiful!
O beautiful! and that seemed more profound
This morning by the pillar when I sat   25

1   The Piazza San Marco.
2   The low pile is the basilica of St Mark, the Campanile is its bell tower, and the
     long ranges of classic chiselling are the colonnades on either side of the square.

Under the great arcade, at the review,[3]
And took, and held, and ordered on my brain
The faces, and the voices, and the whole mass
O' the motley facts of existence flowing by!
O perfect, if 'twere all. But it is not;   30
Hints haunt me ever of a More beyond:
I am rebuked by a sense of the incomplete
Of a completion over-soon assumed
Of adding up too soon. What we call sin
I could believe a painful opening out   35
Of paths for ampler virtue.[4] The bare field,
Scant with lean ears of harvest, long had mocked
The vext laborious farmer. Came at length
The deep plough in the lazy undersoil
Down-driving; with a cry earth's fibres crack,   40
And a few months, and lo! the golden leas,
And autumn's crowded shocks and loaded wains.
Let us look back on life. Was any change,
Any now blest expansion, but at first
A pang, remorse-like, shot to the inmost seats   45
Of moral being? To do anything,
Distinct on any one thing to decide,
To leave the habitual and the old, and quit
The easy-chair of use and wont, seems crime
To the weak soul, forgetful how at first   50
Sitting down seemed so too. Oh, oh, these qualms,
And oh these calls! And oh! this woman's heart,
Fain to be forced, incredulous of choice,
And waiting a necessity for God.

3   The parade of Austrian soldiers.
4   This difficult passage may be seen as an antiphonal response to the soliloquy
    of the previous scene. Whereas then Dipsychus had warned himself against
    premature action, now he insists that he must do more than merely rest in the
    enjoyment of his present idleness – even if the action he takes may conflict with
    conventional morality.

Yet, I could think, indeed, the perfect call   55
Should force the perfect answer. If the voice
Ought to receive its echo from the soul,
Wherefore this silence? If it *should* rouse my being,
Why this reluctance? Have I not thought o'ermuch
Of other men, and of the ways of the world?   60
But what they are, or have been, matters not.
To thine own self be true, the wise man says.[5]
Are then my fears myself? O double self!
And I untrue to both. O there are hours
When love, and faith, and dear domestic ties,   65
And converse with old friends, and pleasant walks,
Familiar faces, and familiar books,
Study, and art, upliftings unto prayer,
And admiration of the noblest things,
Seem all ignoble only; all is mean,   70
And nought as I would have it. Then at others,
My mind is on her nest; my heart at home
In all around; my soul secure in place,
And the vext needle perfect to her poles.
Aimless and hopeless in my life I seem   75
To thread the winding byways of the town
Bewildered, baffled, hurried hence and thence,
All at cross-purpose ever with myself,
Unknowing whence from whither. Then, in a moment,
At a step I crown the Campanile's top   80
And view all mapped below: islands, lagoon,
An hundred steeples and a million roofs,
The fruitful champaign, and the cloud-capt Alps,
And the broad Adriatic. Be it enough;
If I lose this, how terrible! No, no   85
I am contented and will not complain.
To the old paths, my soul! Oh, be it so!
I bear the workday burden of dull life

---

5   Polonius, in Shakespeare's *Hamlet* (I, 3).

About these footsore flags of a weary world
Heaven knows how long it has not been; at once   90
Lo! I am in the spirit on the Lord's day
With John in Patmos.[6] Is it not enough,
One day in seven? and if this should go
If this pure solace should desert my mind
What were all else? I dare not risk this loss.   95
To the old paths, my soul!

Sp.
                              O yes
To moon about religion; to inhume[7]
Your ripened age in solitary walks
For self-discussion; to debate in letters
Vext points with earnest friends; past other men   100
To cherish natural instincts, yet to fear them
And less than any use them. Oh, no doubt,
In a corner sit and mope, and be consoled
With thinking one is clever, while the room
Rings through with animation and the dance.   105
Then talk of old examples, and pervert
Ancient real facts to modern unreal dreams,
And build up baseless fabrics of romance
And heroism upon historic sand;
To burn, forsooth, for Action, yet despise   110
Its merest accidence and alphabet;
Cry out for service, and at once rebel
At the application of its plainest rules:
This you call life, my friend, reality,
Doing your duty unto God and man –   115
I know not what. Stay at Venice, if you will;
Sit musing in its churches hour on hour
Cross-kneed upon a bench; climb up at whiles

---

6   Where St John wrote the Apocalypse, or Book of Revelation (Rev. 1, 9).
7   To bury in the ground.

The neighbouring tower, and kill the lingering day
With old comparisons. When night succeeds,   120
Evading, yet a little seeking, what
You would and would not, turn your doubtful eyes
On moon and stars to help morality.
Once in a fortnight, say, by lucky chance
Of happier-tempered coffee, gain (great Heaven!)   125
A pious rapture: it is not enough?
O that will keep you safe. Yet don't be sure –
Emotions are so slippery. Aye keep close
And burrow in your bedroom; pace up and down
A long half hour; with talking to yourself   130
Make waiters wonder; sleep a bit; write verse,
Burnt in disgust, then ill-restored and left,
Half-made, in pencil scrawl illegible.[8]
Sink ere the end, most like, the hapless prey
Of some chance chambermaid, more sly than fair,   135
And in vain call for me. O well I know
You will not find, when I am not to help
E'en so much face as hires a gondola.
Beware!

Di.
'Tis well; thou cursed spirit, go thy way!   140
I am in higher hands than yours. 'Tis well.
Who taught you menaces? Who told you, pray,
Because I asked you questions, and made show
Of hearing what you answered, therefore –

Sp.
                           Oh
As if I didn't know!

---

8   More than one editor of Clough's verse has observed that this is an accurate
    description of many of the MSS in his *Nachlass*.

Di.

                  Come, come my friend   145
I may have wavered, but I have thought better.
We'll say no more of it.

Sp.

                  Oh, I dare say
But as you like; 'tis our own loss; once more
Beware!

Di. (alone)
Must it be then? So quick upon my thought   150
To follow the fulfilment and the deed?
I counted not on this; I counted ever
To hold and turn it over in my hands
Much longer, much. I took it up indeed,
For speculation rather; to gain thought,   155
New data. Oh, and now to be goaded on
By menaces, entangled amongst tricks!
That I won't suffer. Yet it is the law;
'Tis this makes action always. But for this
We ne'er should act at all; and act we must.   160
Why quarrel with the fashion of a fact
Which, one way, must be; one time, why not now?

Sp.

        Submit! Submit!
        For tell me then, in earth's great laws
        Have you found any saving clause   165
        Exemption special granted you
        From doing what the rest must do?
        Of common sense who made you quit
        And told you, you'd no need of it
        Nor to submit.   170

        To move on angels' wings were sweet

But who would therefore scorn his feet?
It cannot walk up to the sky;
It therefore will lie down and die.
Rich meats it don't obtain at call   175
It therefore will not eat at all.
Poor babe, and yet a babe of wit!
But common sense? Not much of it
Or 'twould submit

Submit, submit!   180
As your good father did before you
And as the mother who first bore you!
O yes! a child of heavenly birth!⁹
But yes it *was* pupped too on earth.
Keep your new birth for that far day   185
When in the grave your bones you lay,
All with your kindred and connection,
In hopes of happy resurrection.
But how meantime to live is fit,
Ask common sense; and what says it?   190
Submit, submit!

'Tis common sense and human wit
Can find no higher name than it.
Submit, submit!

O I am with you, my sweet friend,   195
Yea, always, even to the end.¹⁰

---

9   An allusion to Wordsworth's *Immortality Ode*.
10   Yet another blasphemous allusion by the Spirit to words of Jesus: 'I am with
     you alway, even unto the end of the world' (Mt 28, 20).

Scene 4

Di.
'Tis gone, the fierce inordinate desire,
The burning thirst for Action – utterly;
Gone, like a ship that passes in the night
On the high seas; gone, yet will come again.
Gone, yet expresses something that exists.   5
Is it a thing ordained then? Is it a clue
For my life's conduct? Is it a law for me
That opportunity shall breed distrust
Not passing until that pass? Chance and resolve
Like two loose comets wandering wide in space   10
Crossing each other's orbits time on time,
Meet never. Void indifference and doubt
Let through the present boon, which ne'er turns back
To await the after sure-arriving wish.
How shall I then explain it to myself   15
That in blank thought my purpose lives?
The uncharged cannon mocking still the spark
When come, which *ere* come it had loudly claimed.
Am I to let it be so still? For truly
The need exists, I know; the wish but sleeps   20
(Sleeps and anon will wake and cry for food)
And to put by these unreturning gifts,
Because the feeling is not with me now
Which will I know be with me presently,
Seems folly more than merest babyhood's.   25
But must I then do violence to myself
And push on nature, force desire (that's ill)
Because of knowledge? Which is great, but works
By rules of large exception; to tell which
Naught is more fallible than mere caprice.   30

To use knowledge well we must learn of ignorance:
To apply the rule forget the rule. Ah but
I am compromised, you think. Oh, but indeed
I shan't do it more for that. No! nor refuse
To vindicate a scarce contested right   35
And certify vain independentness.

But what need is there? I am happy now,
I feel no lack – what cause is there for haste?
Am I not happy? is not that enough?

Sp.

        O yes, O yes! and thought, no doubt,   40
        'T had locked the very devil out.
        He, he! He, he! and didn't know
        Through what small places we can go?
        How do, my pretty dear? What! drying
        Its pretty eyes? Has it been crying?   45

Di.
Depart!

Sp.
O yes, you thought you had escaped, no doubt,
This worldly fiend that follows you about,
This compound of convention and impiety
This mongrel of uncleanness and propriety   50
What else were bad enough? But let me say,
I too have my *grandes manières*[1] in my way;
Could speak high sentiment as well as you,
And out-blank-verse you without much ado
Have my religion also in my kind,   55
For dreaming unfit, because not designed.
What! you know not that I too can be serious,

1   Grand manners.

Can speak big words, and use the tone imperious;
Can speak, not honeydly of love and beauty
But sternly of a something much like duty?   60
O, do you look surprised? were never told
Perhaps, that all that glitters is not gold?[2]
The Devil oft the Holy Scripture uses,
But God can act the Devil when he chooses.
Farewell! But *verbum sapienti satis*[3] –   65
I do not make this revelation gratis.
Farewell: beware.

Di.
> Off, devil, leave me

Sp.
>   Devil, oh!
> And how the devil can you know
> Whether a devil I am or no?   70
> Some of you think, I'm told, there's none
> How should you think that I am one?
> Why, *le bon dieu*,[4] who when all's done
> Like other people likes his fun
> In black his angels often dresses   75
> Which much all tender souls distresses
> That daren't for anything act on guesses.
> They stop, they moan, they whine, while he
> Sits chuckling up above to see.
> How can your qualms so chill and shivery   80
> Prove I'm not a cherub out of livery –
> For aught your silly conscience knows
> The Angel Gabriel in plain clothes?
> O, by their fruits you know them. Well

---

2   Cf. Shakespeare's *Merchant of Venice*, Act II, Scene 7.
3   'To the wise a word is enough', a proverbial expression.
4   The good God.

Are you so sure that you can tell   85
What in fact are the good fruits – eh?
The sacred scriptures surely say
The second person of the Trinity
When living here not in divinity
By every Jewish godly liver   90
Was thought a glutton and wine bibber
Indeed, so bad was his behaviour
Beelzebub[5] they called our Saviour
Much as occasionally you please
To call me Mephistopheles.   95
Nay, can you swear I'm not your soul –
The better half, if not the whole
Still offering you a word in season –
The embodiment of your perfect reason.

Di.
What, loitering still? Still, O foul spirit, there?   100
Go hence, I tell thee, go! I *will* beware.

(alone)
It must be then. I feel it in my soul
The iron enters, sundering flesh and bone,
And sharper than the two-edged sword of God.
I come into deep waters – help, O help!   105
The floods run over me.

Therefore, farewell! A long and last farewell
Ye pious sweet simplicities of life,
Good books, good friends, and holy moods and all
That lent rough life sweet Sunday-seeming rests,   110
Making earth heaven-like. Welcome, wicked world,
The hardening heart, the calculating brain
Narrowing its doors to thought, the lying lips,

---

5   A name for the devil, meaning in Hebrew 'Lord of the Flies'.

The calm-dissembling eyes; the greedy flesh,
The world, the Devil – welcome, welcome, welcome![6]   115

> *(from within)*
> The stern Necessity of things
> On every side our being rings;
> Our sallying eager actions fall
> Vainly against that iron wall.
> Where once her finger points the way,   120
> The wise think only to obey;
> Take life as she has ordered it,
> And come what may of it, submit
> Submit, submit!

> Who take implicitly her will   125
> For these her vassal-chances still
> Bring store of joys, successes, pleasures
> But who so ponders, weighs and measures,
> She calls her torturers up to goad
> With spur and scourges on the road;   130
> He does at last with pain whate'er
> He spurned at first. Of such beware,
> Beware, beware!

Di.
O God, O God! The great floods of the fiend
Flow over me! I come into deep waters   135
Where no ground is![7]

Sp.
                    Don't be the least afraid
There's not the slightest reason for alarm.

6   Users of the Book of Common Prayer, in the Litany, pray 'from all the deceits
    of the world, the flesh, and the devil, Good Lord deliver us'.
7   Cf Psalm 69, 1–2: 'Save me O God: for the waters are come in, even to my soul.
    / I stick fast in the deep mire, where no ground is'.

I only meant by a perhaps rough shake
To rouse you from a dreamy, unhealthy sleep.
Up, then – up, and be going: the large world   140
The thronged life awaits us.
      Come, my pretty boy
You've been making mows[8] to the blank sky
Quite long enough for good. We'll put you up
Into the higher form. 'Tis time you learn
The Second Reverence,[9] for things around.   145
Up, then, and go amongst them; don't be timid
Look at them quietly a bit: by-and-by
Respect will come, an healthy appetite
So let us go.
     How now! not yet awake?
Oh, you will sleep yet, will you! Oh, you shirk   150
You try and slink away! You cannot, eh?
Nay now, what folly's this? Why will you fool yourself?
Why will you walk about thus with your eyes shut,
Treating for facts the self-made hues that float
On tight-pressed pupils, which you know are not facts?   155
To use the undistorted light of the sun
Is not a crime; to look straight out upon
The big plain things that stare one in the face
Does not contaminate; to see pollutes not
What one must feel if one won't see; what *is*   160
And will be too, howe'er we blink, and must
One way or other make itself observed.
Free walking's better than being led about; and
What will the blind man do, I wonder, if
Some one should cut the string of his dog? Just think   165
What could you do, if I should go away?

8 Gloomy grimaces, as in 'mop and mow'.
9 An allusion to Carlyle's translation of Goethe's novel *Wilhelm Meister*: 'Then
 comes the second: Reverence for what is under us'.

O, you have paths of your own before you, have you?
What shall it take to? literature, no doubt?
Novels, reviews? or poems if you please!
The strong fresh gale of life will feel, no doubt,   170
The influx of your mouthful of soft air.
Well, make the most of that small stock of knowledge
You've condescended to receive from me;
That's your best chance. Oh you despise that! Oh
Prate then of passions you have known in dreams,   175
Of huge experience gathered by the eye;
Be large of aspiration, pure in hope,
Sweet in fond longings, but in all things vague.
Breathe out your dreamy scepticism, relieved
By snatches of old songs. People will like that, doubtless   180
Or will you write about philosophy?
For a waste far off *maybe* overlooking
The fruitful *is* close by, live in metaphysic
With transcendental logic fill your stomach,
Schematise joy, effigiate meat and drink;   185
Or, let me see, a mighty Work, a Volume,
The Complemental of the inferior Kant,[10]
The critic of Pure Practic, based upon
The antinomies of the Moral Sense; for, look you,
We cannot act without assuming x,   190
And at the same time y, its contradictory;
Ergo, to act. People will buy that, doubtless.
Or you'll perhaps teach youth (I do not question
Some downward turn you may find, some evasion
Of the broad highway's glaring white ascent),   195
Teach youth – in a small way; that is, always

---

10 'Transcendental' (beyond experience), 'schematise' (organise in a pattern), 'effigiate' (form into shape) and 'antinomy' (a pair of contradictory propositions derived from the same premises) are all technical terms of the philosophy of Immanuel Kant. Kant had written a *Critique of Pure Reason* and a *Critique of Practical Reason*. A *Critique of Pure Practic* would no doubt trump them both.

So as to have much time left for yourself;
This you can't sacrifice, your leisure's precious.
Heartily you will not take to anything;
Will parents like that, think you? 'He writes poems,   200
He's odd opinions – hm! – and's not in Orders' –
For that you won't be. Well, old college fame,
The charity of some free-thinking merchant,
Or friendly intercession brings a first pupil;
And not a second. Oh, or if it should,   205
Whatever happen, don't I see you still
Living no life at all? Even as now
An o'ergrown baby, sucking at the dugs
Of Instinct, dry long since. Come, come, you are old enough
For spoon-meat[11] surely.   210
                                    Will you go on thus
Until death end you? If indeed it does.
For what it does, none knows. Yet as for you,
You'll hardly have the courage to die outright;
You'll somehow halve even it. Methinks I see you,
Through everlasting limbos of void time,   215
Twirling and twiddling ineffectively,
And indeterminately swaying for ever.
Come, come, spoon-meat at any rate.
                                    Well, well
I will not persecute you more, my friend
Only, do think, as I observed before   220
What *can* you do, if I should go away?

Di.
Is the hour here, then? Is the minute come –
The irreprievable instant of stern time?
O for a few, few grains in the running glass,
Or for some power to hold them![12] O for a few   225

11 Solid baby-food.
12 An echo of the last words of Faust in Marlowe's *Doctor Faustus*.

Of all that went so wastefully before!
It must be then, e'en now!

> (*from within*)

>> It must, it must.
>> 'Tis Common Sense! and human wit
>> Can claim no higher name than it.   230
>> Submit, submit!

>> Necessity! and who shall dare
>> To bring to *her* feet excuse or prayer
>> Beware, beware!
>> We must, we must   235
>> Howe'er we turn and pause and tremble –
>> Howe'er we shrink, deceive, dissemble –
>> Whate'er our doubting, grief, disgust,
>> The hand is on us and we must
>> We must, we must.   240
>> 'Tis common sense! and human wit
>> Can find no better name than it.
>> Submit, submit!

>> Fear not, my lamb, whate'er men say
>> I am the Shepherd, and the Way.[13]   245

---

13 Once more the Spirit allocates to himself descriptions ascribed in the Gospels
to Christ (John 10, 14 and 14, 6).

Scene 5

Di.

Twenty-one past, twenty-five coming on
One third of life departed, nothing done.[1]
Out of the Mammon of Unrighteousness
That we make friends, the Scripture is express.[2]
   Mephisto, come; we will agree.   5
   Content; you'll take a moiety.

Sp.

   A moiety, ye gods, he he!

Di.

   Three quarters then. One eye you close
   And lay your finger to your nose.
   Seven eighths? nine tenths? O griping beast 10
   Leave me a decimal at least.

Sp.

   Oh, one of ten! to infect the nine
   And make the devil a one be mine.
   Oh, one, to jib all day, God wot,
   When all the rest would go full trot!   15
   One very little one, eh? to doubt with
   Just to pause, think, and look about with?
   In course! you counted on no less –
   You thought it likely I'd say yes!

1 Clough was in fact 31 at the time of the dramatic date of Dipsychus.
2 The mammon of unrighteousness, with which Jesus ironically told his disciples to make friends, is money unscrupulously come by.

Di.
Be it then thus – since that it must, it seems.   20
Welcome, O world, henceforth; and farewell dreams!
Yet know, Mephisto, know, nor you nor I
Can in this matter either sell or buy;
For the fee simple[3] of this trifling lot
To you or me, trust me, pertaineth not.   25
I can but render what is of my will,
And behind it somewhat remaineth still.
Oh, your sole chance was in the childish mind
Whose darkness dreamed that vows like this could bind;
Thinking all lost, it made all lost, and brought   30
In fact the ruin which had been but thought.
Thank Heaven (or you!) that's past these many years,
And we have knowledge wiser than our fears.
                    So your poor bargain take, my man
                    And make the best of it you can.   35

Sp.

                    With reservations! oh how treasonable!
                    When I had let you off so reasonable.
                    However, I don't fear; be it so!
                    Brutus is honourable, I know;[4]
                    So mindful of the dues of others   40
                    So thoughtful for his poor dear brothers,
                    So scrupulous, considerate, kind –
                    He wouldn't leave the devil behind
                    If he assured him he had claims
                    For his good company to hell-flames!   45
                    No matter, no matter, the bargain's made
                    And I for my part will not be afraid.
                    Little Bo Peep, she lost her sheep

---

3   Unconditional tenure.
4   So Mark Antony describes Caesar's assassin Brutus in his famous speech in
    Shakespeare's *Julius Caesar*.

> And knew not where to find them.[5]
> He, he, with reservations, Christo!   50
> A child like you to cheat Mephisto!
> With reservations, oh! ho! ho!
> But time, my friend, has yet to show
> Which of us two will closest fit
> The proverb of the Biter Bit.   55
> Little Bo Peep , she lost her sheep –

Di.
Tell me thy name, now it is over.

Sp.

> Oh!
> Why, Mephistopheles, you know –
> At least, you've lately called me so;
> Belial it was some days ago.   60
> But take your pick: I've got a score
> Never a royal baby more.
> For a brass plate upon a door
> What think you of *Cosmocrator*?[6]

Di.
Tous kosmokratoras tou aiwnos toutou,[7]   65
And that you are indeed, I do not doubt you.

Sp.

> Ephesians, ain't it? near the end
> You dropt a word to spare your friend.

---

5   Here the children's nursery rhyme is placed in juxtaposition to the Gospel simile of the Good Shepherd.
6   Ruler of the world.
7   Dipsychus quotes in Greek part of a passage from the Epistle to the Ephesians which speaks of the Christian's struggle against 'the rulers of the darkness of this world and spiritual wickedness in high places'.

What follows, too, in application
Would be absurd exaggeration.   70

Di.
The Power of this World! hateful unto God!

Sp.

Cosmarchon's[8] shorter, but sounds odd.
One wouldn't like, even if a true devil
To be taken for a vulgar Jew devil.

Di.
Yet in all these things we – 'tis Scripture too –   75
Are more than conquerors, even over you.[9]

Sp.

Come, come, don't maunder[10] any longer
Time tests the weaker and the stronger
And we, without procrastination,
Must set, you know, to our vocation.   80
O goodness; won't you find it pleasant
To own the positive and present;
To see yourself like people round
And feel your feet upon the ground!

Little Bo Peep, she lost her sheep!   85

(Aside)

In the Piazza di San Marco

---

8   Another Greek word for 'ruler of the world'. It is not clear why it is thought to
    sound like a Jewish name.
9   The Scripture is Rom. 8, 37: 'we are more than conquerors through him that
    loved us'.
10 Ramble.

O won't I try him after dark, oh
Oh Jesus Christ! It will be funny
If I don't get my earnest money.[11]

(Exeunt ambo)

11　The Spirit long ago placed a bet that he would succeed as a tempter, and now
　　that Dipsychus has submitted to the world and the devil there is no reason
　　why he should not enjoy the pleasures of the flesh on offer in the Piazza.

SEVEN SONNETS

I

That children in their loveliness should die
Before the dawning beauty, which we know
Cannot remain, has yet begun to go;
That when a certain period has passed by,
People of genius and of faculty,
Leaving behind them some result to show,
Having performed some function, should forego
A task which younger hands can better ply,
Appears entirely natural. But that one
Whose perfectness did not at all consist
In things towards forming which time could have done
Anything, – whose sole office was to exist –
Should suddenly dissolve and cease to be
Is the extreme of all perplexity.

Seven Sonnets

II

That there are better things within the womb
Of Nature than to our unworthy view
She grants for a possession, may be true:
The cycle of the birthplace and the tomb
Fulfils at least the order and the doom
Of earth, that has not ordinance to do
More than to withdraw and to renew,
To show one moment and the next resume:
The law that we return from whence we came
May for the flowers, beasts, and most men remain;
If for ourselves, we ask not nor complain:
But for a being that demands the name
We highest deem – a Person and a Soul –
It troubles us if this should be the whole.

III

To see the rich autumnal tints depart,
And view the fading of the roseate glow
That veils some Alpine altitude of snow,
To hear some mighty masterpiece of art
Lost or destroyed, may to the adult heart,
Impatient of the transitory show
Of lovelinesses that but come and go,
A positive strange thankfulness impart.
When human pure perfections disappear,
Not at the first, but at some later day,
The buoyancy of such reaction may
With strong assurance conquer blank dismay.

IV

But whether in the uncoloured light of truth
This inward strong assurance be, indeed,
More than the self-willed arbitrary creed,
Manhood's inheritor to the dream of youth;
Whether to shut out fact because forsooth
To live were insupportable unfreed,

Be or be not the service of untruth;
Whether this vital confidence be more
Than his, who upon death's immediate brink
Knowing, perforce determines to ignore;
Or than the bird's, that when the hunter comes
Burying her eyesight, can forget her fear;
Who about this shall tell us what to think?

V

If it is thou whose casual hand withdraws
What it at first as casually did make,
Say what amount of ages it will take
With tardy rare concurrences of laws
And subtle multiplicities of cause,
The thing they once had made us to remake;
May hopes dead-slumbering dare to reawaken
E'en after utmost interval of pause?
What revolutions must have passed, before
The great celestial cycles shall restore
The starry sign whose present hour is gone;
What worse than dubious chances interpose,
With cloud and sunny gleam to recompose
The skiey picture we had gazed upon.

VI

But if, as (not by what the soul desired
Swayed in the judgement) wisest men have thought,
And (furnishing the evidence it sought)
Man's heart hath ever fervently required,
And story, for that reason deemed inspired,
To every clime, in every age, hath taught;
If in this human complex there be aught
Not lost in death, as not in birth acquired,
O then, though cold the lips that did convey
Rich freights of meaning, dead each living sphere
Where thought abode and fancy loved to play
Thou, yet we think, somewhere somehow still art,
And satisfied with that the patient heart
The where and how doth not desire to hear.

VII

Shall I decide it by a random shot?
Our happy hopes, so happy and so good,
Are not mere idle motions of the blood;
And when they seem most baseless, most are not.
A seed there must have been upon the spot
Where the flowers grow, without it ne'er they could.
The confidence of growth least understood
Of some deep intuition was begot.
What if despair and hope alike be true?
The heart, 'tis manifest, is free to do
Whatever Nature and itself suggest
And always 'tis a fact that we are here;
And with being here, does palsy-giving fear
(Whoe'er can ask?), or hope accord the best?

SONGS IN ABSENCE

Ye flags of Piccadilly,
　　　Where I posted up and down
And wished myself so often
　　　Well away from you and town, –

Are the people walking quietly
　　　And steady on their feet
Cabs and omnibuses plying
　　　Just as usual in the street?

Do the houses look as upright
　　　As of old they used to be,
And does nothing seem affected
　　　By the pitching of the sea?

Through the Green Park iron railings
　　　Do the quick pedestrians pass?
Are the little children playing
　　　Round the plane-tree in the grass?

This squally wild north-wester
　　　With which our vessel fights,
Does it merely serve with you to
　　　Carry up some paper kites?

Ye flags of Piccadilly,
　　　Which I hated so, I vow
I would wish with all my heart
　　　You were underneath me now!

Where lies the land to which the ship would go?
Far, far ahead, is all her seamen know.
And where the land she travels from? Away,
Far, far behind, is all that they can say.

On sunny noons upon the deck's smooth face,
Linked arm in arm, how pleasant here to pace;
Or, o'er the stern reclining, watch below
The foaming wake far widening as we go.

On stormy nights when wild north-westers rave,
How proud a thing to fight with wind and wave!
The dripping sailor on the reeling mast
Exults to bear, and scorns to wish it past.

Where lies the land to which the ship would go?
Far, far ahead, is all her seamen know.
And where the land she travels from? Away,
Far, far behind, is all that they can say.

MARI MAGNO
or
TALES ON BOARD

A youth was I. An elder friend with me,
'Twas in September o'er the autumnal sea
We went; the wide Atlantic ocean o'er
Two amongst many the strong steamer bore.
    Delight it was to feel that wondrous force
That held us steady to our purposed course,
The burning resolute victorious will
'Gainst winds and waves that strive unwavering still.
Delight it was with each returning day
To learn the ship had won upon her way
Her sum of miles, – delight were mornings grey
And gorgeous eves, – nor was it less delight,
On each more temperate and favouring night,
Friend with familiar or with new-found friend,
To pace the deck, and o'er the bulwarks bend,
And the night watches in long converse spend;
While still new subjects and new thoughts arise
Amidst the silence of the seas and skies.
    Amongst the mingled multitude a few,
Some three or four, towards us early drew;
We proved each other with a day or two;
Night after night some three or four we walked
And talked, and talked, and infinitely talked.
    Of the New England ancient blood was one;
His youthful spurs in letters he had won,
Unspoilt by that, to Europe late had come, –
Hope long deferred, – and went unspoilt by Europe home.
What racy tales of Yankeeland he had.

Up-country girl, up-country farmer lad;
The regnant clergy of the time of old
In wig and gown; – tales not to be retold
By me. I could but spoil were I to tell:
Himself must do it who can do it well.

An English clergyman came spick and span
In black and white – a large well favoured man,
Fifty years old, as near as one could guess.
He looked the dignitary more or less.
A rural dean,[1] I said, he was, at least,
Canon perhaps; at many a good man's feast
A guest had been, amongst the choicest there.
Manly his voice and manly was his air:
At the first sight you felt he had not known
The things pertaining to his cloth alone.
Chairman of Quarter Sessions[2] had he been?
Serious and calm, 'twas plain he much had seen,
Had miscellaneous large experience had
Of human acts, good, half and half, and bad.
Serious and calm, yet lurked, I know not why,
Sometimes a softness in his voice and eye.
Some shade of ill a prosperous life had crossed;
Married no doubt; a wife or child had lost?
He never told us why he passed the sea.

My guardian friend was now, at thirty-three,
A rising lawyer – ever, at the best,
Slow rises worth in lawyer's gown compressed;
Succeeding now, yet just, and only just
His new success he never seemed to trust.
By nature he to gentlest thoughts inclined,
To most severe had disciplined his mind;
He held it duty to be half unkind.
Bitter, they said, who but the exterior knew;

---

1   A cleric supervising a group of parochial clergy.
2   A local court with civil and criminal jurisdiction, held once a quarter.

In friendship never was a friend so true:
The unwelcome fact he did not shrink to tell,
The good, if fact, he recognised as well.
Stout to maintain, if not the first to see;
In conversation who so great as he?
Leading but seldom, always sure to guide,
To false or silly, if 'twas borne aside,
His quick correction silent he expressed,
And stopped you short, and forced you to your best.
Often, I think, he suffered from some pain
Of mind that on the body worked again;
One felt it in his sort of half-disdain,
Impatient not, but acrid in his speech;
The world with him her lesson failed to teach
To take things easily and let them go.
      He, for what special fitness I scarce know,
For which good quality, or if for all,
With less of reservation and recall
And speedier favour than I e'er had seen,
Took, as we called him, to the rural dean.
As grew the gourd, as grew the stalk of bean,
So swift it seemed, betwixt these differing two
A stately trunk of confidence up-grew.
      Of marriage long one night they held discourse,
Regarding it in different ways, of course.
Marriage is discipline, the wise had said,
A needful human discipline to wed;
Novels of course depict it final bliss, –
Say, had it ever really once been this?
      Our Yankee friend (whom, ere the night was done,
We called New England or the Pilgrim Son),
A little tired, made bold to interfere
'Appeal,' he said 'to me; my sentence hear.
You'll reason on till night and reason fail;
My judgement is you each shall tell a tale;
And as on marriage you can not agree,

Of love and marriage let the stories be.'
Sentence delivered, as the younger man,
My lawyer friend was called on and began.
    '*Infandum jubes!*[3] 'tis of long ago
If tell I must, I tell the tale I know:
Yet the first person using for the freak,
Don't rashly judge that of myself I speak.'
So to his tale; if of himself or not
I never learnt, we thought so on the spot.
Lightly he told it as a thing of old,
And lightly I repeat it as he told.

THE LAWYER'S FIRST TALE
Primitiae, or Third Cousins

1

'Dearest of boys, please come to-day,
Papa and Mama have bid me say,
They hope you'll dine with us at three;
They will be out till then, you see,
But you will start at once, you know,
And come as fast as you can go.
Next week they hope you'll come and stay
Some time, before you go away.
Dear boy, how pleasant it will be,
Ever your dearest Emily!'
    Twelve years of age was I, and she
Fourteen, when thus she wrote to me,
A schoolboy, with an uncle spending
My holidays, then nearly ending.
My uncle lived the mountain o'er

---

3   A truncated quotation of Aeneas' response to Dido when she asks him to tell the tale of the fall of Troy: 'You ask me, Queen, to revisit unspeakable grief' (Virgil, *Aeneid*, II, 3).

A rector, and a bachelor.
The vicarage was by the sea
That was the home of Emily:
The windows to the front looked down
Across a single-streeted town
Far as to where Worms-head was seen,
Dim with ten watery miles between;
The Carnedd mountains on the right
With lofty masses filled the sight;
To left, the open sea; the bay
In a blue plain before you lay.[4]
 A garden, full of fruit, extends,
Stone-walled, above the house, and ends
With a locked door, that by a porch
Admits to churchyard and to church;
Farm-buildings nearer on one side,
And glebe, and then the country wide.
 I and my cousin Emily
Were cousins in the third degree;
My mother near of kin was reckoned
To hers, who was my mother's second:
My cousinship I held from her.
Such an amount of girls there were,
At first one really was perplexed.
'Twas Patty first, and Lydia next,
And Emily the third, and then
Philippa, Phoebe, Mary Gwen.
Six were they, you perceive, in all;
And portraits fading on the wall,
Grandmothers, heroines of old,
And aunts of aunts, with scrolls that told
Their names and dates, were there to show
Why these had all been christened so.

---

4 The description of the scenery makes clear that the vicarage was located in
Beaumaris, with a view towards Great Orme ('Worms-head').

Mari Magno

The crowd of blooming daughters fair
Scarce let you see the mother there,
And by her husband, large and tall,
She looked a little shrunk and small;
Although my mother used to tell
That once she was a county belle:
Busied she seemed, and half-distress'd
For him and them to do the best.
    The vicar was of bulk and thews,
Six feet he stood without his shoes,
And every inch of all a man;
Ecclesiast on the ancient plan,
Unforced by any party rule
His native character to school;
In ancient learning not unread,
But had few doctrines in his head;
Dissenters truly he abhorred,
They never had his gracious word.
He ne'er was bitter or unkind,
But positively spoke his mind.
Their piety he could not bear,
A sneaking, snivelling set they were:
Their tricks and meanness fired his blood;
Up for his Church he stoutly stood.
No worldly aim had he in life
To set him with himself at strife;
A spade a spade he freely named,
And of his joke was not ashamed,
Made it and laughed at it, be sure,
With young and old, and rich and poor.
His sermons frequently he took
Out of some standard reverend book;
They seemed a little strange, indeed,
But were not likely to mislead.
Others he gave that were his own,
The difference could be quickly known.

110

Mari Magno

Though sorry not to have a boy
His daughters were his perfect joy;
He plagued them, oft drew tears from each,
Was bold and hasty in his speech;
All through the house you heard him call,
He had his vocatives for all:
Patty Patina, Pat became,
Lydia took Languish with her name,
Philippa was the Gentle Queen,
And Phoebe Madam Proserpine
The pseudonyms for Mary Gwen
Varied with every week again;
But Emily, of all the set,
Emilia called, was most the pet.

    Soon as her messenger had come,
I started from my uncle's home,
On an old pony scrambling down
Over the mountain to the town.
My cousins met me at the door,
And some behind, and some before,
Kissed me all round and kissed again,
The happy custom there and then
From Patty down to Mary Gwen.

    Three hours we had, and spent in play
About the garden and the hay;
We sat upon the half-built stack;
And when 'twas time for hurrying back,
Slyly away the others hied,
And took the ladder from the side;
Emily there, alone with me,
Was left in close captivity;
But down the stack at last I slid
And found the ladder they had hid.

    I left at six; again I went
Soon after and a fortnight spent:
Drawing, by Patty I was taught

To music I could not be brought;
I showed them how to play at chess,
I argued with the governess;
I called them stupid; why to me
'Twas evident as A B C;
Were not the reasons such and such?
      Helston, my schoolfellow, but much
My senior, in a yacht came o'er,
His uncle with him, from the shore
Under Worms-head: to take a sail
He pressed them, but could not prevail;
Mama was timid, durst not go,
Papa was rather gruff with no.
Helston no sooner was afloat,
We made a party in a boat
And rowed to Sea-Mew Island out,
And landed there and roved about:
And I and Emily out of reach
Strayed from the rest along the beach.
Turning to look into a cave
She stood, when suddenly a wave
Ran up; I caught her by the frock
And pulled her out, and o'er a rock
So doing, stumbled, rolled, and fell.
She knelt down, I remember well,
Bid me where I was hurt to tell,
And kissed me three times as I lay;
But I jumped up and limped away.
The next was my departing day.
      Patty arranged it all with me
To send next year to Emily
A valentine. I wrote and sent;
For the fourteenth it duly went.
On the fourteenth what should there be
But one from Emily to me;
The postmark left it plain to see.

Mine, though they praised it at the time,
Was but a formal piece of rhyme.
She sent me one that she had bought;
'Twas stupid of her, as I thought:
Why not have written one? She wrote,
However, soon, this little note.

    'Dearest of boys, of course 'twas you;
You printed, but your hand I knew,
And verses too, how did you learn?
I can't send any in return.
Papa declares they are not bad –
That's praise from him – and I'm so glad,
Because you know no one can be
I'd rather have to write to me.

    'Our governess is going away
We're so distressed she cannot stay:
Mama had made it quite a rule
We none of us should go to school.
But what to do they do not know,
Papa protests it must be so.
Lydia and I may have to go;
Patty will try to teach the rest,
Mama agrees it will be best.
Dear boy, good-bye, I am, you see,
Ever your dearest Emily,
We want to know, so write and tell,
If you'd a valentine as well.'

II

Five tardy years were fully spent
Ere next my cousins' way I went;
With Christmas then I came to see
My uncle in his rectory:
But they the town had left; no more

Were in the vicarage of yore.
When time his sixtieth year had brought
An easier cure the vicar sought:
A country parsonage was made
Sufficient, amply, with the aid
Of mortar here and there, and bricks
For him and wife and children six.
Though neighbours now, there scarce was light
To see them and return ere night.
      Emily wrote: how glad they were
To hear of my arrival there;
Mama had bid her say that all
The house was crowded for the ball
Till Tuesday, but if I would come,
She thought that they could find me room;
The week with them I then should spend,
But really must the ball attend;
'Dear cousin, you have been away
For such an age, pray don't delay
But come and do not lose a day.'
      A schoolboy still, but now, indeed,
About to college to proceed,
Dancing was, let it be confessed,
To me no pleasure at the best:
Of girls and of their lovely looks
I thought not, busy with my books.
Still, though a little ill-content,
Upon the Monday morn I went.
My cousins each and all I found
Wondrously grown! They kissed me round,
And so affectionate and good
They were, it could not be withstood.
Emily, I was so surprised,
At first I hardly recognised;
Her face so formed and rounded now,
Such knowledge in her eyes and brow;

For all I read and thought I knew,
She could divine me through and through.
Where had she been, and what had done,
I asked, such victory to have won?
She had not studied, had not read,
Seemed to have little in her head,
Yet of herself the right and true,
As of her own experience, knew.
Straight from her eyes her judgments flew,
Like absolute decrees they ran,
From mine on such a different plan.
      A simple county country ball
It was to be, not grand at all;
And cousins four with me would dance,
And keep me well in countenance.
And there were people there to be
Who knew of old my family,
Friends of my friends – I heard and knew,
And tried; but no, it would not do,
Somehow it seemed a sort of thing
To which my strength I could not bring;
The music scarcely touched my ears,
The figures fluttered me with fears.
I talked, but had not aught to say,
Danced, my instructions to obey;
E'en when with beautiful good-will
Emilia through the long quadrille
Conducted me, alas the day,
Ten times I wished myself away.
      But she, invested with a dower
Of conscious, scarce-exerted power,
Emilia, so, I know not why,
They called her now, not Emily,
Amid the living, heaving, throng,
Sedately, somewhat, moved along,
Serenely, somewhat, in the dance

Mingled, divining by a glance,
And reading every countenance;
Not stately she, nor grand, nor tall,
Yet looked as if controlling all
The fluctuations of the ball;
Her subjects ready at her call
All others, she a queen, her throne
Preparing and her title known,
Though not yet taken as her own.
O wonderful! I still can see,
And twice she came and danced with me.
     She asked me of my school, and what
Those prizes were that I had got,
And what we learnt, and 'oh', she said,
'How much to carry in one's head!'
And I must be upon my guard,
And really must not work too hard:
Who were my friends? And did I go
Ever to balls? I told her, no:
She said, 'I really like them so
But then I am a girl; and, dear,
You like your friends at school, I fear,
Better than anybody here.'
How long had she left school, I asked
Two years, she told me, and I tasked
My faltering speech to learn about
Her life, but could not bring it out:
This while the dancers round us flew.
     Helston, whom formerly I knew,
My schoolfellow, was at the ball,
A man full-statured, fair and tall,
Helston of Helston now, they said,
Heir to his uncle, who was dead;
In the army, too: he danced with three
Of the four sisters. Emily
Refused him once, to dance with me.

How long it seemed! And yet at one
We left, before 'twas nearly done:
How thankful I! The journey through
I talked to them with spirits new;
And the brief sleep of closing night
Brought a sensation of delight,
Which, when I woke, was exquisite.
The music moving in my brain
I felt; in the gay crowd again
Half felt, half saw the girlish bands,
On their white skirts their white-gloved hands,
Advance, retreat, and yet advance,
And mingle in the mingling dance.
The impulse had arrived at last,
When the opportunity was past.
    Breakfast my soft sensations first
With livelier passages dispersed.
Reposing in his country home,
Which half luxurious had become,
Gay was their father, loudly flung,
His guests and blushing girls among,
His jokes; and she their mother, too,
Less anxious seemed, with less to do,
Her daughters aiding. As the day
Advanced, the others went away,
But I must absolutely stay,
The girls cried out. I stayed and let
Myself be once more half their pet
Although a little on the fret.
    How ill our boyhood understands
Incipient manhood's strong demands!
Boys have such troubles of their own
As none, they think, have ever known,
Religious, social, of all kinds
That tear and agitate their minds.
A thousand thoughts within me stirred

Mari Magno

Of which I could not speak a word;
Strange efforts after something new,
Which I was wretched not to do;
Passions, ambitions lay and lurked,
Wants, counter-wants, obscurely worked
Without their names and unexplained.
And where had Emily obtained
Assurance, and had ascertained?
How strange, how far behind was I,
And how it came, I asked, and why?
How was it, and how could it be,
And what was all that worked in me?

      They used to scold me when I read,
And bade me talk to them instead;
When I absconded to my room,
To fetch me out they used to come;
Oft by myself I went to walk,
But, by degrees, was got to talk.

      The year had cheerfully begun
With more than winter's wonted sun;
Mountains, in the green garden ways,
Gleamed through the laurels and the bays.
One day, as there I looked about,
I well remember letting out,
While they of girls discoursing sat
This one how sweet, how lovely that,
That I could greater pleasure take
In looking on Llynidwil lake[5]
Than on the fairest female face:
They could not understand: a place!
Incomprehensible it seemed;
Philippa looked as if she dreamed,

---

5   Llyn Idwal is a small isolated lake six miles north-east of Snowdon. Local tradition says that no bird will fly over it, since a legendary prince was drowned there by his stepfather.

118

Patty and Lydia loud exclaimed,
And I already was ashamed,
When Emily asked, half apart,
If to the lake I'd given my heart;
And did the lake, she wished to learn,
My tender sentiment return.
For music, too, I would not care,
Which was an infinite despair:
When Lydia took her seat to play,
I took a book, or walked away.
  I was not quite composed, I own,
Except when with the girls alone;
Looked to their father still with fear
Of how to him I must appear;
And was entirely put to shame
When once some rough he-cousins came;
Yet Emily from all distress
Could reinstate me, more or less;
How pleasant by her side to walk,
How beautiful to let her talk!
How charming! Yet by slow degrees,
I got impatient, ill at ease;
Half glad, half wretched, when at last
The visit ended, and 'twas past.

III

Next year I went and spent a week,
And certainly had learnt to speak;
My chains I forcibly had broke
And now too much indeed I spoke.
  A mother sick and seldom seen
A grief for many weeks had been.
Their father too was feebler, years
Were heavy, and there had been fears

119

Some months ago; and he was vexed
With party heats and all perplexed
With an upheaving modern change
To him and his old wisdom strange.
The daughters all were there, not one
Had yet to other duties run.
Their father, people used to say,
Frightened the wooers all away; –
As vines around an ancient stem
They clung and clustered upon him,
He loved and tended; above all,
Emilia, ever at his call.
But I was – intellectual.
     I talked in a superior tone
Of things the girls had never known,
Far wiser to have let alone;
Things which the father knew in short
By country-clerical report;
I talked of much I thought I knew
Used all my college wit anew,
A little on my fancy drew;
Religion, politics, O me!
No subject great enough could be.
In vain, more weak in spirits grown,
At times he tried to put me down.
     I own it was the want, in part,
Of any discipline of heart.
It was, now hard at work again,
The busy argufying brain
Of the prize schoolboy; but indeed,
Much more, if right the cause I read,
It was the instinctive wish to try
And, above all things, not be shy.
     Alas! It did not do at all;
Ill went the visit, ill the ball.
Each hour I felt myself grow worse,

With every effort more perverse.
I tried to change; too hard, indeed,
I tried and never could succeed.
Out of sheer spite an extra day
I stayed; but when I went away
Alas, the farewells were not warm,
The kissing was the merest form;
Emilia was *distraite* and sad,
And everything was bad as bad.

O had some happy chance fall'n out,
To turn the thing just round about
In time at least to give anew
The old affectionate adieu!
A little thing, a word, a jest
A laugh, had set us all at rest;
But nothing came. I went away,
And could have really cried that day,
So vexed, for I had meant so well,
Yet everything so ill befell,
And why and how I could not tell.

Our wounds in youth soon close and heal,
Or seem to close; young people feel,
And suffer greatly, I believe,
But then they can't profess to grieve:
Their pleasures occupy them more,
And they have so much time before.
At twenty life appeared to me
A sort of vague infinity;
And though of changes still I heard,
Real changes had not yet occurred:
And all things were, or would be, well,
And nothing irremediable.
The youth for his degree that reads
Beyond it nothing knows or needs;

Nor till 'tis over wakes to see
The busy world's reality.

One visit brief I made again
In autumn next but one, and then
All better found. With Mary Gwen
I talked, a schoolgirl just about
To leave this winter and come out.
Patty and Lydia were away,
And a strange sort of distance lay
Betwixt me and Emilia.
She sought me less, and I was shy.
       And yet this time I think that I
Did subtly feel, more saw, more knew
The beauty into which she grew;
More understood the meanings now
Of the still eyes and rounded brow,
And could, perhaps, have told you how
The intellect that crowns the race
To more than beauty in her face
Was changed. But I confuse from hence
The later and the earlier sense.

IV

Have you the Giesbach seen?[6] A fall
In Switzerland, you say, that's all;
That and an inn, from which proceeds
A path that to the Faulhorn leads,
From whence the world you see of snows.
Few see how perfect in repose,
White green, the lake lies deeply set,
Where, slowly purifying yet,

6   A stream and waterfall on the south side of Lake Brienz.

The icy river-floods retain
A something of the glacier stain.
Steep cliffs arise the waters o'er;
The Giesbach leads you to a shore,
And to one still sequestered bay
I found elsewhere a scrambling way.
Above, the loftier heights ascend,
And level platforms here extend
The mountains and the cliffs between,
With firs and grassy spaces green,
And little dips and knolls to show
In part or whole the lake below;
And all exactly at the height
To make the pictures exquisite.
          Most exquisite they seemed to me
When, a year after my degree,
Passing upon my journey home
From Greece and Sicily and Rome,
I staid at that minute hotel
Six days, or eight, I cannot tell.
          Twelve months had led me fairly through
The old world surviving in the new.
From Rome with joy I passed to Greece,
To Athens and the Peloponnese;
Saluted with supreme delight
The Parthenon-surmounted height;
In huts at Delphi made abode,
And in Arcadian valleys rode;
Counted the towns that lie like slain
Upon the wide Boeotian plain;
With wonder in the spacious gloom
Stood of the Mycenian tomb;
From the Acrocorinth watched the day
Light the eastern and the western bay.
Constantinople then had seen,
Where, mid her cypresses, the queen

Of the East sees flow through an entrance wide
The steady streaming Scythian tide.[7]
And after, from Scamander's mouth
Went up to Troy, and to the south,
To Lycia, Caria, pressed, at whiles
Outvoyaging to Egean isles: –
      To see the things which, sick with doubt
And comment, one had learnt about,
Was like clear morning after night,
Or raising of the blind to sight.
Aware it might be first and last,
I did it eagerly and fast,
And took unsparingly my fill.
The impetus of travel still
Urged me, – but laden, half oppressed,
Here lighting on a place of rest,
I yielded, asked not if 'twere best.
      Pleasant it was, reposing here,
To sum the experience of the year,
And let the accumulated gain
Assert itself upon the brain.
Travel's a miniature life
Travel is evermore a strife,
Where he must run who would obtain.
'Tis a perpetual loss and gain;
For sloth and error dear we pay,
By luck and effort win our way,
And both have need of, every day.
Each day has got its sight to see,
Each hour must put to profit be;
Pleasant, when seen are all the sights,
To let them think themselves to rights.
I on the Giesbach turf reclined,

---

7   These verses recapitulate the itinerary of the spring tour through Greece and Turkey recorded by Clough in the 1861 diary in which he also scribbled the first draft of this poem.

Half watched this process in my mind;
Watched the streams purifying slow,
In me and in the lake below;
And began then to think of home,
And possibilities to come.

Brienz on our Brienzer See
From Interlaken every day
A steamer seeks, and at our pier
Lets out a crowd to see things here;
Up a steep path they pant and strive;
When to the level they arrive,
Dispersing, hither, thither, run,
For all must rapidly be done,
And seek, with questioning and din,
Some the cascade, and some the inn;
The waterfall, for if you look,
You find it printed in the book
That man or woman, so inclined,
May pass the very fall behind,
So many feet there intervene
The rock and flying jet between;
The inn, 'tis also in the plan,
(For tourist is a hungry man)
And a small *salle* repeats by rote
A daily task of *table d'hôte*,
Where broth and meat, and country wine,
Assure the strangers that they dine;
Do it they must while they have power,
For in three-quarters of an hour
Back comes the steamer from Brienz,
And with one clear departure hence
The quietude is more intense.
                It was my custom at the top
To stand and see them clambering up,
Then take advantage of the start,

And pass into the woods apart.
        It happened, and I know not why,
I once returned too speedily;
And seeing women still and men,
Was swerving to the woods again
But for a moment stopped to seize
A glance at someone by the trees;
A figure full, but full of grace,
Its movement beautified the place.
It turns, advances, comes my way;
What do I see, what do I say?
Yet to a statelier beauty grown,
It is, it can be, she alone!
O mountains round! O heaven above!
It is – Emilia, whom I love;
'Emilia, whom I love,' the word
Rose to my lips, as yet unheard,
When she, whose colour flushed to red,
Half turned, and soft, 'my husband' said;
And Helston came up with his hand,
And both of them took mine; but stand
And talk they could not, they must go;
The steamer rang her bell below;
How curious that I did not know;
They were to go and stay at Thun,
Could I come there and see them soon?
And shortly were returning home,
And when would I to Helston come?
Thus down we went, I put them in;
Off went the steamer with a din,
And on the pier I stood and eyed
The bridegroom seated by the bride,
Emilia closing to his side.

V

She wrote from Helston; begged I'd come
And see her in her husband's home.
I went, and bound by double vow,
Not only wife, but mother now,
I found her, lovely as of old,
Or rather, lovelier manifold.

      Her wifely sweet reserve unbroken,
Still frankly, tenderly, she spoke;
Asked me about myself, would hear
What I proposed to do this year;
At college why was I detained,
Was it the fellowship I'd gained?

      I told her that I was not tied
Henceforward further to reside,
Yet very likely might stay on,
And lapse into a college don;
My fellowship itself would give
A competence on which to live,
And if I waited, who could tell,
I might be tutor too, as well.[8]

      Oh, but, she said, I must not stay,
College and school were only play;
I might be sick, perhaps, of praise,
But must not therefore waste my days!
Fellows grow indolent, and then
They may not do as other men,
And for your happiness in life
Sometime you'll wish to have a wife.

      Languidly by her chair I sat,
But my eyes rather flashed at that.

8   In the first part of the nineteenth century the fellows of Oxford colleges ('dons')
were not, as such, obliged to teach. Some of them were appointed as tutors,
which brought teaching duties and extra emoluments.

I said 'Emilia, people change,
And yet, I own, I find it strange
To hear this common talk from you:
You speak, and some believe it true,
Just as any wife would do;
Whoe'er one takes, 'tis much the same,
And love – and so forth, but a name.'
    She coloured 'What can I have said,
Or what could put it in your head?
Indeed, I had not in my mind
The faintest notion of the kind.'
    I told her that I did not know –
Her tone appeared to mean it so.
'Emilia, when I've heard,' I said,
'How people match themselves and wed
I've sometimes wished that both were dead.'

    She turned a little pale. I woke
Some thought; what thought? But soft she spoke:
'I'm sure that what you meant was good,
But really you misunderstood:
From point to point so quick you fly,
And are so vehement, – and I,
As you remember long ago
Am stupid; certainly am slow.
And yet some things I seem to know;
I know it will be just a crime
If you should waste your powers and time.
There is so much, I think, that you,
And no one equally, can do.'
'It does not matter much,' said I,
'The things I thought of are gone by;
I'm quite content to wait to die.'

    A sort of beauteous anger spread
Over her face. 'O me!' she said,

'That you should sit and trifle so,
And you so utterly don't know
How greatly you have yet to grow,
How wide your objects have to expand,
How much is yet an unknown land!
You're twenty three, I'm twenty five,
And I am so much more alive.'
      My eyes I shaded with my hand,
And almost lost my self-command.
I muttered something: 'Yes, I see
Two years have severed you from me.
O Emily, was it ever told,'
I asked 'that souls are young and old?'
      But she, continuing, 'All the day
Were I to speak, I should but say
The one same thing the one same way.
Sometimes, indeed, I think you know,'
And her tone suddenly was low,
'That in a day we yet shall see,
You of my sisters and of me,
And of the things that used to be,
Will think, as you look back again,
With something not unlike disdain.
So you your rightful place obtain,
That will to me be joy, not pain.'
Her voice still lower, lower fell,
I heard, just heard, each syllable.
'But,' in the tone she used before,
Don't stay at college any more!
For others it perhaps may do,
I'm sure it will be bad for you.'

      She softened me. The following day
We parted. As I went away
Her infant on her bosom lay,
And, as a mother might her boy,

I think she would with loving joy
Have kissed me; but I turned to go,
'Twas better not to have it so.
        Next year achieved me some amends,
And once we met, and met as friends,
Friends yet apart; I had not much
Valued her judgement, though to touch
Her words had power; yet strangely still,
It has been cogent on my will.
As she had counselled, I had done,
And a new effort was begun.
Forth to the war of life I went
Courageous, and not ill content.

'Yours is the fault I opened thus again
A youthful, ancient, sentimental vein,'
He said, 'and like Munchausen's[9] horn o'erflow
With liquefying tunes of long ago.
My wiser friend, who knows for what we live,
And what should seek, will his correction give.'
        We all made thanks. 'My tale were quickly told,'
The other said, 'but the turned heavens behold;
The night two watches of the night is old,
The sinking stars their suasions urge for sleep.
My story till to-morrow night will keep.'

The Second Night

The evening after, when the day was stilled,
His promise thus the clergyman fulfilled.

9   Baron Munchausen was an eighteenth-century German soldier who narrated
    absurdly exaggerated exploits.

Mari Magno

THE CLERGYMAN'S FIRST TALE
Love is Fellow-Service

A youth and maid upon a summer night
Upon the lawn, while yet the skies were light
Edmund and Emma, let their names be these,
Among the shrubs within the circling trees,
Joined in a game with boys and girls at play:
For games perhaps too old a little they;
In April she her eighteenth year begun
And twenty he, and near to twenty-one.
A game it was of running and of noise;
He as a boy, with other girls and boys
(Her sisters and her brothers), took the fun;
And when her turn, she marked not, came to run,
'Emma', he called – then knew that he was wrong,
Knew that her name to him did not belong.
Her look and manner proved his feeling true, –
A child no more, her womanhood she knew.
Half was the colour mounted on her face,
Her tardy movement had an adult grace.
Vexed with himself, and shamed, he felt the more
A kind of joy he ne'er had felt before.
Something there was that from this date began,
'Twas beautiful with her to be a man.

Two years elapsed, and he, who went and came,
Changing in much, in this appeared the same;
The feeling, if it did not greatly grow,
Endured and was not wholly hid below.
He now, o'er tasked at school, a serious boy,
A sort of after-boyhood to enjoy
Appeared – in vigour and in spirit high
And manly grown, but kept the boy's soft eye:
And full of blood, and strong and light of limb,
To him 'twas pleasure now to ride, to swim;

The peaks, the glens, the torrents tempted him.
Restless, it seemed, – long distances would walk,
And lively was, and vehement in talk.
A wandering life his life had lately been,
Books he had read, the world had little seen.
One former frailty haunted him, a touch
Of something introspective overmuch.
With all his eager motions still there went
A self-correcting and ascetic bent,
That from the obvious good still led astray
And set him travelling on the longest way;
Seen in these scattered notes their date that claim
When first that feeling conscious sought a name.

   'Beside that wishing-gate which so they name,[10]
'Mid northern hills to me this fancy came,
A wish I formed, my wish I thus expressed:
Would I could wish my wishes all to rest,
And know to wish the wish that were the best!
O for some winnowing wind, to the empty air
This chaff of easy sympathies to bear
Far off, and leave me of myself aware!
While thus this over-health deludes me still,
So willing that I know not what I will,
O for some friend, or more than friend, austere,
To make me know myself, and make me fear!
O for some touch, too noble to be kind,
To wake to life the mind within the mind!'
   'O charms, seductions and divine delights,
All through the radiant yellow summer nights,
Dreams, hardly dreams, that yield or e'er they're done
To the bright fact, my day, my risen sun!

10 In the Lake District, one mile from Grasmere Church, near Wordsworth's
Cottage, is the Wishing Gate at which, according to Baddeley's *Guide*, 'the least
superstitious will not begrudge a few minutes' halt for the sake of the beau-
tiful view'.

O promise and fulfilment, both in one!
O bliss, already bliss, which nought has shared,
Whose glory no fruition has impaired,
And, emblems of my state, thou coming day,
With all thy hours unspent to pass away!
Why do I wait? What more propose to know?
Where the sweet mandate bids me, let me go;
My conscience in my impulse let me find,
Justification in the moving mind,
Law in the strong desire; or yet behind,
Say, is there aught the spell that has not heard,
A something that refuses to be stirred?'
    'Vain were my fancies, empty was my fear,
Not wholly fond, not simply kind she were,
Not soft indulgence all: I see it well,
Rejoicing I have seen, she can repel.
In youthful fervour when, and youthful heat
I came – to be rejected was so sweet,
To be repulsed so grateful. O to love
Who knows, must know to turn our steps above!'[11]
    'In other regions has my being heard
Of a strange language the diviner word?
Has some forgotten life the exemplar shown,
As dooms me here, in this, to live alone?[12]
Thou, love, that shouldest blind me, let me, love
Nothing behold beyond thee or above;
Ye impulses, that should be strong and wild,
Beguile me, if I am to be beguiled!'
    'Or are there modes of love, and different kinds
Proportioned to the sizes of our minds?
There are who say thus. I held there was one,

---

11 The preceding eight lines occur only in a manuscript: they were omitted from the 1869 edition on the grounds that they were too obscure.

12 At this point in the MS occur the following three lines: 'This hesitance, that lets me not fulfil / My own desires, – divine? Or is it still / A flux of thinking, and a waste of will?'

One love, one deity, one central sun.
As he resistless brings the expanding day,
So love should come on his victorious way.
If light at all, can light indeed be there
Yet only permeate half the ambient air,
Can the high noon be regnant in the sky
Yet half the land in light and half in darkness lie?
Can love, if love, be occupant in part,
Hold, as it were, some chambers in the heart;
Tenant at will of so much of the soul,
Not lord and mighty master of the whole?
There are who say, and say that it is well;
Opinion all, of knowledge none can tell.'
       'Montaigne, I know, in a realm high above
Places the seat of friendship over love;
'Tis not in love that we should think to find
The lofty fellowship of mind with mind;
Love's not a joy where soul and soul unite
Rather a wondrous animal delight;
And as in spring for one consummate hour
The world of vegetation turns to flower,
The birds with liveliest plumage trim their wing,
And all the woodland listens as they sing;
When spring is o'er and summer days are sped,
The songs are silent and the blossoms dead:
E'en so of man and woman is the bliss.
O, but I will not tamely yield to this!
I think it only shows us in the end,
Montaigne was happy in a noble friend,
Had not the fortune of a noble wife;
He lived, I think, a poor ignoble life,
And wrote of petty pleasure, petty pain;
I do not greatly think about Montaigne.'[13]

---

13 The sentiments that Edmund rejects are expressed in the twenty-eighth chapter
    of the first book of Montaigne's essays.

'How charming to be with her! yet indeed
After a while I find a blank succeed;
After a while she little has to say,
I'm silent too, although I wish to stay;
What would it be all day, day after day?
Ah, but I ask, I do not doubt, too much
I think of love as if it should be such
As to fulfil and occupy in whole
The nought-else-seeking, nought-essaying soul.
Therefore it is my mind with doubts I urge,
Hence are these fears and shiverings on the verge;
By books, not nature, thus have we been schooled,
By poetry and novels been befooled;
Wiser tradition says, the affections' claim
Will be supplied, the rest will be the same.
I think too much of love, 'tis true: I know
It is not all, was ne'er intended so;
Yet such a change, so entire, I feel, 'twould be,
So potent, so omnipotent with me,
My former self I never should recall, –
Indeed I think it must be all in all.'
            'I thought that love was winged; without a sound
His purple pinions bore him o'er the ground,
Wafted without an effort here or there,
He came – and we too trod as if in air: –
But panting, toiling, clambering up the hill,
Am I to assist him? I, put forth my will
To upbear his lagging footsteps, lame and slow,
And help him on and tell him where to go,
And ease him of his quiver and his bow?'   .
        '*Erotion!*[14] I saw it in a book;
Why did I notice it, why did I look?
Yea, is it so, ye powers that see above?
I do not love, I want, I try to love!

14 *Erotion* is a Greek name for a little Cupid.

This is not love, but lack of love instead!
Merciless thought! I would I had been dead,
Or e'er the phrase had come into my head!'

She also wrote: and here may find a place,
Of her and of her thoughts some slender trace.

   'He is not vain; if proud, he quells his pride,
And somehow really likes to be defied;
Rejoices if you humble him: indeed
Gives way at once, and leaves you to succeed.'
   'Easy it were with such a mind to play,
And foolish not to do so, some would say;
One almost smiles to look and see the way:
But come what will, I will not play a part,
Indeed I dare not condescend to art.'
   'Easy 'twere not, perhaps, with him to live;
He looks for more than anyone can give:
So dulled at times and disappointed; still
Expecting what depends not of my will:
My inspiration comes not at my call,
Seek me as I am, if seek you do at all.'
   'Like him I do, and think of him I must;
But more – I dare not and I cannot trust.
This more he brings – say, is it more or less
Than that, no fruitage ever came to bless –
The old wildflower of love-in-idleness?'
   'Me when he leaves and others when he sees,
What is my fate who am not there to please?
Me he has left; already may have seen
One, who for me forgotten here has been;
And he, the while, is balancing between.
If the heart spoke, the heart I know were bound;
What if it utter an uncertain sound?'
   'So quick to vary, so rejoiced to change,
From this to that his feelings surely range;

His fancies wander and his thoughts as well,
And if the heart be constant, who can tell?
Far off to fly, to abandon me, and go
He seems, returning then before I know:
With every accident he seems to move
Is now below me and is now above,
Now far aside, – O, does he really love?'
      'Absence were hard; yet let the trial be;
His nature's aim and purpose he would free,
And in the world his course of action see.
O should he lose, not learn; pervert his scope!
O should I lose! And yet to win I hope.
I win not now; his way if now I went,
Brief joy I gave, for years o discontent.'
      'Gone, is it true? But oft he went before,
And came again before a month was o'er.
Gone – though I could not venture upon art,
It was perhaps a foolish pride in part;
He had such ready fancies in his head,
And really was so easy to be led;
One might have failed; and yet I feel 'twas pride
And can't but half repent I never tried.
Gone, is it true? But he again will come,
Wandering his loves, and loves returning home.'

      Gone, it was true; nor came so soon again;
Came after travelling, pleasure half, half pain.
Came, but a half of Europe first o'erran;
Arrived, his father found a ruined man.
Rich they had been, and rich was Emma too,
Heiress of wealth she knew not, Edmund knew.
      Farewell to her! – In a new home obscure,
Food for his helpless parents to secure
From early morning to advancing dark
He toiled and laboured as a merchant's clerk.
Three years his heavy load he bore, nor quailed,

Then all his health, though scarce his spirit, failed;
Friends interposed, insisted it must be,
Enforced their help, and sent him to the sea.
      Wandering about, with little here to do,
His old thoughts mingling dimly with his new,
Wandering one morn, he met upon the shore,
Her whom he quitted five long years before.
      Alas! Why quitted? Say that charms are nought,
Nor grace, nor beauty worth one serious thought,
Was there no mystic virtue in the sense
That joined your boyish girlish innocence?
Is constancy a thing to throw away,
And loving faithfulness a chance of every day?
Alas! Why quitted? Is she changed? But now
The weight of intellect is in her brow:
Changed, or but truer seen, one sees in her
Something to wake the soul, the interior sense to stir.
      Alone they met, from alien eyes away,
The high shore hid them in a tiny bay.
Alone was he, was she; in sweet surprise
They met, before they knew it, in their eyes.
In his a wondering admiration glowed,
In hers a world of tenderness o'erflowed;
In a brief moment all was known and seen
That of slow years the wearying work had been
Morn's early odorous breath perchance in sooth,
Awoke the old natural feeling of their youth:
The sea, perchance, and solitude had charms,
They met – I know not – in each other's arms.
      Why linger now – why waste the sands of life?
A few sweet weeks, and they were man and wife.

      To his old frailty do not be severe:
His latest theory with patience hear:

      'I sought not, truly, would to seek disdain, –

138

A kind, soft pillow for a wearying pain,
Fatigues and cares to lighten, to relieve;
But love is fellow-service, I believe.'
    'No, truly not, it was not to obtain,
Though that perchance were happiness, were gain,
A tender breast to fall upon and weep,
A heart, the secrets of my heart to keep
To share my hopes, and in my griefs to grieve;
Yet love is fellow-service, I believe.'
    'Yet in the eye of life's all-seeing sun
We shall behold a something we have done,
Shall of the work together we have wrought,
Beyond our aspiration and our thought,
Some not unworthy issue yet receive;
For love is fellow-service I believe.'

    The tale, we said, instructive was, but short;
Could he not give another of the sort?
He feared his second might his first repeat,
'And Aristotle teaches, change is sweet.
You my defect more fitly could complete,'
He added, turning to New England's son
'And close what we at your desire begun.'
'The briefest of the brief is mine,' said he,
'Accept it, if accepted it can be.'

THE AMERICAN'S TALE
Or Juxtaposition

This incident, I have been told, befell
Once in a huge American hotel.
    Two sisters slept together in one bed.
The elder, suffering with an aching head,

Early retired: the younger, late who came,
Found her asleep; in haste to be the same,
Undressed, but ready into bed to go,
Her watch remembered in a room below.
Just-robed she slipped away; with silent pace
Returned, she thought, and took her usual place
And slept, nor woke the sleeper by her laid.
The sun was shining high, ere woke the maid;
At once she woke, and waking, wondering eyed
In bed upseated, gazing, at her side
A youth: – her error flashed upon her mind,
And from the stranger's bed her own to find
Just-robed, she fled, and left her watch behind.
        Easy in a row of twenty rooms or more
At night to be deceived about a door.
        One quarter of a morning hour had sped
While he the maiden slumbering in his bed
Silent had viewed: and he had nothing said
Or sought to say to appease her waking fright
Or to retard a moment of her flight.
The watch he took; it marked not noonday yet,
Its owner in the garden when he met
Swift he went up and almost ere she knew
Swift in her hands he placed it, swift withdrew.
        I know not how it was, my tale affirms
That after this they met on happy terms,
And love, that lives by accident, they say,
And scorns occasion offering every day,
Love, from this accident, it seems, arose,
Love and a happy marriage were the close.
Who told me this, a lady, said she knew.

        My friend 'Of many,' said, 'I call it true,
Of marriage, as of treason, one may say
We do not seek, we find it on our way.'
        'Yet,' said the clergyman, 'we have a voice,

And choose, altho' restricted is our choice.
In its degrees and kinds I hold that love
Is all about, beneath us, and above;
Love to no station and no race confined,
Tho' rule, convenience, chance our unions bind
One knows not where one does or does not find.'
    Said he who told the story, 'Will you say
Love to unite them did but take this way?
Love begins not when lovers meet and kiss,
They were intended for each other's bliss
When souls began: what do we know of this?
Something there is, to which a statesman grave
Vague title of *Superior Order* gave;
Something subsists behind each petty deed,
Each casual-seeming chance, which is indeed
The fact from whence our showy facts proceed.
But come, our younger friend in this dim night
Under his bushel must not hide his light.'
I said I'd had but little time to live
Experience none or confidence could give;
'But I can tell to-morrow, if you please,
My last year's journey towards the Pyrenees.'
To-morrow came, and evening, when it closed
The penalty of speech on me imposed.

The Third Night

MY TALE
A la banquette, or a Modern Pilgrimage

I waited at La Queille, ten miles or more
From the old-Roman sources of Mont Dore;
Travellers to Tulle this way have got to go;
An old high road from Lyons to Bordeaux;

141

From Tulle to Brives the swift Corrèze descends,
At Brives you've railway and your trouble ends.[15]
A little *bourg* La Queille; and from the height
The mountains of Auvergne are all in sight;[16]
Green pastoral heights, that once in lava flowed,
Of primal fire the product and abode,
And all the plateaux and the lines that trace
Where in deep dells the waters find their place;
Far to the south above the lofty plain
The Plomb de Cantal lifts his towering train.[17]
A little after one with little fail
Down drove the diligence that bears the mail;
The *courier* therefore called, in whose *banquette*
A place I got, and thankful was to get:
The new postillion climbed his seat, *allez*,
Off broke the four cart-horses on the way,
Westward we roll o'er heathy backs of hills,
Crossing the future rivers in the rills;
Bare table-lands are these, and sparsely sown,
Turning their waters south to the Dordogne.
        Close-packed we were, and little at our ease,
The *conducteur* impatient with the squeeze;
Not tall he seemed, but bulky round about,
His cap and jacket made him look more stout;
In *grande tenue* he rode of *conducteur*;[18]
Black eyes he had, black his moustaches were,

15 The places mentioned are all in the Auvergne region of central France. They
    would occur on the first stages of a 'journey towards the Pyrenees' from Mont-
    Dore, such as Clough undertook in 1861.
16 Clough's MS contains at this point the two following lines: 'The Puy de Sancy
    and the Puy de Dome, / Were Puy on Puy, you'd see the gates of Rome'.
17 Clough's MS contains at this point the lines 'Ascend the steep and you may
    see the show; / Mid-day was burning, and I did not go'.
18 The *courier* is the mail coach, the *conducteur* is the uniformed coachman, the
    postillion sits beside him on the near side, and the *banquette* is the bench for
    passengers.

Shaven his chin, his hair and whiskers cropt;
A ready man; at Ussel when we stopt
For me and for himself, bread, meat, and wine,
He got, the *courier* did not wait to dine;
To appease our hunger, and allay our drouth
We ate and took the bottle at the mouth;
One draught I had, the rest entire had he;
For wine his body had capacity.
　　A peasant in his country *blouse* was there,
He told me of the *conseil* and the *maire*.[19]
Their *maire*, he said, could neither write nor read,
And yet could keep the registers, indeed;
The *conseil* had resigned – I know not what, –
Good actions here are easily forgot:
He in the *quarante-huit* had something done,[20]
Were things but fair, some notice should have won.
　　A *militaire*, a soldier on sick leave,
In uniform, unmarked upon the sleeve,
There was; the *conducteur*, I know not why,
Among the trunks behind us made him lie.
By swift Corrèze his home; he did not know
Where he could sleep and how he was to go,
Feeble he seemed and nothing had to say
And fumbled with his papers as he lay.
I questioned him, but little answer drew.
Pock-marked he was, I hoped it was not new.[21]
　　Another youth there was, a soldier he,
A soldier ceasing with today to be;
Three years had served, for three had bought release;
From war returning to the arts of peace,
To Tulle he went, as his department's town,

19　The *conseil* was the mayor's legal adviser.
20　The revolution of 1848 which deposed Louis Philippe and led eventually to
　　the Second Empire of Napoleon III.
21　This paragraph was omitted from the 1869 edition, presumably because of the
　　reference to syphilis.

To-morrow morn to pay his money down.
    In Italy, his second year begun,
This youth had served, when Italy was won.
He told of Montebello, and the fight
That ended fiercely with the close of night.[22]
There was he wounded, fell and thought to die,
Two Austrian cones had passed into his thigh;
One traversed it, the other, left behind,
In hospital the doctor had to find:
At eight of night he fell, and sadly lay
Till three of morning on the following day,
When peasant came and put him on a wain,
And drove him to Voghera in his pain;
To Alessandria thence the railway bore,
In Alessandria then two months and more
He lay in hospital; to lop the limb
The Italian doctor who attended him
Was much disposed, but high above the knee;
For life an utter cripple he would be.
Then came the typhoid fever, and the lack
Of food. And sick and hungering, on his back,
With French, Italians, Austrians as he lay,
Arrived the tidings of Magenta's day,
And Milan entered in the burning June,
And Solferino's issue following soon.[23]
Alas, the glorious wars! And shortly he
To Genoa for the advantage of the sea,
And to Savona, suffering still, was sent
And joined his now returning regiment.
Good were the Austrian soldiers, but the feel

22 In 1859 Napoleon III went to war with Austria and invaded Italy. Montebello near Pavia (now Montebello della battaglia) was the scene of an early engagement during this campaign.
23 French victories over the Austrians at Magenta and Solferino led to the Austrians ceding Lombardy to Napoleon, who handed it over to the Savoy monarchy – a crucial stage in the Italian Risorgimento.

They did not well encounter of cold steel,
Nor in the bayonet fence of man with man
Maintained their ground, but yielded, turned and ran.
Les armes blanches and the rifled gun
Had fought the battles and the victories won.
The glorious wars! But he, the doubtful chance
Of soldier's glory quitting and advance,
His wounded limb less injured than he feared, –
Was dealing now in timber, it appeared;
Oak-timber finding for some mines of lead,
Worked by an English company, he said.
This youth perhaps was twenty-three years old;
Simply and well his history he told.
    They wished to hear about myself as well;
I told them, but it was not much to tell;
At the Mont Dore, of which the guide-book talks,
I'd taken, not the waters, but the walks.
Friends I had met, who on their southward way
Had gone before, I followed them today.
    They wondered greatly at this wondrous thing, –
Les Anglais are for ever on the wing.
The *conducteur* said everybody knew
We were descended of the Wandering Jew.
And on with the declining sun we rolled,
And woods and vales and fuller streams behold.
    About the hour when peasant-people sup,
We dropped the peasant, took a *curé* up,
In hat and bands and *soutane* all to fit.
He next the *conducteur* was put to sit,
I in the corner gained the senior place;
Brown was his hair, but closely shaved his face;
To lift his eyelids did he think it sin?
Older he was, but looked like twenty-two
Fresh from the cases, to the country new.
    The *conducteur*, the *curé* at his side
At once a twinkle in his eyes I spied.

He begged to hear about the pretty pair
Whom he supposed he had been marrying there;
The deed he hoped was comfortably done, –
Monsieur l'Evêque[24] he called him in his fun:
And lifted soon his voice for all to hear;
A baritone he had both strong and clear:
In fragments first of music made essay,
And tried his pipes and modest felt his way.
La verre en main la mort nous trouvera,
It was, or *Ah je dirai à maman!*
And then, *A toi ma belle, à toi toujours*[25]
Till, of his organ's quality secure
Trifling no more, but boldly, like a man,
He filled his chest and gallantly began.

The *conducteur*'s song

'Though I have seemed, against my wiser will,
Your victim, O ye tender foibles, still,
Once now for all, though half my heart be yours,
Adieu, sweet faults, adieu, ye gay amours!
Sad if it be, yet true it is to say,
I've fifty years, and 'tis too late a day,
My limbs are shrinking and my hair turns grey;
Adieu, gay loves, it is too late a day!
    Once in your school (what good, alas! is once?)
I took my lessons and was not the dunce.
O what a pretty girl was then Juliette!
Don't you suppose that I remember yet
Though thirty years divide me from the day
When she and I first looked each other's way?
But now! Midwinter to be matched with May!

24 'My Lord Bishop'.
25 The titles of the songs mean 'Death will find us with a glass in our hand', 'I will tell mother', 'To you, my lovely, always to you'.

Adieu, gay loves, it is too late a day!
      You lovely Marguerite! I shut my eyes
And do my very utmost to be wise;
Yet see you still; and hear, though closed my ears,
And think I'm young in spite of all my years;
Shall I forget you, if I go away?
To leave is painful, but absurd to stay;
I've fifty dreadful reasons to obey.
Adieu, gay loves, it is too late a day!'

      This priest beside this lusty *conducteur*
Under his beaver sat and looked demure;
Faintly he smiled the company to please,
And folded held his hands above his knees.
Then, a propos of nothing, had we heard,
He asked, about a thing that had occurred
At the Mont Dore a little time ago,
A wondrous cure? And when we answered, No,
About a little girl he told a tale,
Who, when her medicines were of no avail,
Was by the doctor ordered to Mont Dore,
But nothing gained and only suffered more.
This little child had in her simple way
Unto the Blessed Virgin learnt to pray,
And, as it happened, to an image there
By the roadside one day she made her prayer,
And of our Lady, who can hear on high,
Begged for her parents' sake she might not die.
Our Lady of Grace, whose attribute is love,
Beheld this child and listened from above.
Her parents noticed from that very day
Her malady began to pass away,
And but a fortnight after, as they tell,
They took her home rejoicing, sound and well.
Things come, he said, to show us every hour
We are surrounded by superior power.

147

Little we notice, but if once we see,
The seed of faith will grow into a tree.
The *conducteur*, he wisely shook his head,
Strange things do happen in our time, he said;
If the *bon Dieu* but please, no doubt indeed,
When things are desperate, yet they will succeed.
Ask the postillion here, and he can tell
Who cured his horse, and what of it befell.

      Then the postillion, in his smock of blue,
His pipe into his mouth's far corner drew,
And told about a farrier and a horse;
But his *Auvergnat* grew from bad to worse;
His rank Arvenian *patois* was so strong,
With what he said I could not go along;
And what befell and how it came to pass,
And if it were a horse or if an ass,
The sequence of his phrase I could not keep
And in the middle fairly sank to sleep.
When I awoke, I heard a stream below
And on each bank saw houses in a row,
Corrèze the stream, the houses Tulle, they said:
Alighted here and thankful went to bed.

      'But how,' said one, 'about the Pyrenees?
In Hamlet give us Hamlet, if you please;
Your friend declares you said you met with there
A peasant beauty, beauteous past compare,
Who fed her cows the mountain peaks between,
And asked if at Velletri you had been;
And was Velletri larger or was Rome?[26]
Her soldier-brother went away from home,
Two years ago, – to Rome it was he went,
And to Velletri was this summer sent;

26 From 1861 to 1870 the Papal States were defended by a French garrison from
the march of the Risorgimento. Velletri is a small town in the Alban hills to the
south-east of Rome.

Mari Magno

He twenty-three, and she was sweet seventeen,
And fed her cows the mountain peaks between.
Lightly along a rocky path she led,
And from a grange she brought you milk and bread.
In summer here she lived, and with the snow
Drove in October to the fields below;
And where you lived, she asked, and oh, they say,
That with the English we shall fight some day;
Loveliest of peasant girls that e'er was seen,
Feeding her cows the mountain peaks between.'
          ''Tis true,' I said 'though to betray was mean.
My Pyrenean verses will you hear,
Though not about that peasant girl, I fear?'
          'Begin,' they said 'the sweet bucolic song,
Though it to other maids and other cows belong,

Currente Calamo

Quick, painter, quick, the moment seize
Amid the snowy Pyrenees;
More evanescent than the snow
The pictures come, are seen, and go:
Quick, quick, *currente calamo*.[27]
          I do not ask the tints that fill
The gate of day, 'twixt hill and hill,
I ask not for the hues that fleet
Above the distant peaks, my feet
Are on a poplar-bordered road
Where with a saddle and a load
A donkey, old and ashen grey,
Reluctant works his dusty way.
Before him, still with might and main
Pulling his rope, the rustic rein,
A girl: before both him and me,
Frequent she turns and lets me see

27 'With rapid pen'.

Unconscious, lets me scan and trace
The sunny darkness of her face
And outlines full of southern grace.
        Following I notice yet and yet
Her olive skin, dark eyes deep set,
And black, and blacker e'en than jet,
The escaping hair, that scantly showed,
Since o'er it in the country mode,
For winter warmth and summer shade,
The lap of scarlet cloth is laid.
And then back-falling from the head
A crimson kerchief overspread
Her jacket blue, thence passing down
A skirt of darkest yellow-brown,
Coarse stuff, allowing to the view
The smooth limb to the woollen shoe.
But who – ? Here's someone following too, –
        A priest, and reading at his book!
Read on, O priest, and do not look;
Consider – she is but a child, –
Yet might your fancy be beguiled.
Read on, O priest, and pass and go!
But see, succeeding in a row,
Two, three, and four, a motley train,
Musicians wandering back to Spain;
With fiddle and with tambourine,
A man with women following seen;
What dresses! ribbon-ends and flowers,
And, sight to wonder at for hours,
The man – to Phillip has he sat?[28] –
With butterfly-like velvet hat;
One dame his big bassoon conveys,
On one his gentle arm he lays;
They stop, and look, and something say,

28 John Phillip RA (1817–67) painted many scenes in Spain, and became known
    as 'Spanish Phillip'.

150

And to 'España' ask the way.
    But while I speak, and point them on,
Alas, my dearer friends are gone;
The dark-eyed maiden and the ass
Have had the time the bridge to pass.
Vainly beyond it far descried,
Adieu, and peace with you abide
Grey donkey, and your beauteous guide.
    The pictures come, the pictures go,
Quick, quick, *currente calamo.*

They praised the rhymes, but still would persevere
The eclogue[29] of the mountain peaks to hear,
Eclogue that never was; and then awhile
Of France, and Frenchmen, and our native isle
They talked; pre-insular above the rest,
My friend his ardent politics expressed;
France was behind us all, he saw in France
Worst retrogression, and the least advance;
Her revolutions had but thrown her back,
Powerful just now, but wholly off the track;
They in religion were, as I had seen,
About where we in Chaucer's time had been;
In Chaucer's time! And yet their Wickliffe where?
Something they'd kept – the worst part – of Voltaire.
    Strong for Old England was New England too;
The clergyman was neutral in his view;
And I for France with more than I could do,
Though sound, my thesis did not long maintain.
The contemplation of the nightly main,
The vaulted heavens above, and under these
The black ship working through the dusky seas
Deserting, to our narrow berths we crept;
Sound slumbered there, the watch while others kept.

29 A short pastoral dialogue poem, often amatory.

Mari Magno

The Fourth Night

An officer of Engineers, and round
By Halifax to far Bermuda bound,
Joined us this night; a rover he had been.
Many strange sights and many climes had seen
And of our stories when he heard us tell
Offered to give a narrative as well.

THE OFFICER'S STORY

To the Crimea when I went[30]
I offered quarters in my tent
To an old man with whiskers gray
And a brown wig, and let him stay
For long: he laughed and played the fool,
Was like a boy released from school
An amateur to see the war
He came, he said, what reason for
Beside, if any were, who knows?
One would have said that soft repose
At home were more the thing for him
Than peril there of life and limb
Where often truly shot and shell
Made something like an earthly hell.
I knew his friends – a junior he
Of an old wealthy family –
His fortune freely still he spent,
Where'er his fancy led him went,
And when his every debt was paid
And every best arrangement made
Had left himself at sixty-one

---

30 In 1854, in the course of a war against Russia, a British and French expeditionary force was sent to the Crimea.

152

Scarce half enough to live upon.
     Returning from the front one day
We found our hero on the way
A woman holding to his arm –
He'd bid her take it in the alarm –
Some blackguard Frenchmen eight or nine
Before him as it were in line;
And he gesticulating quick
And even flourishing his stick
And something finding still to say
To keep them more or less at bay.
     The French retreated as we came
He followed them with cries of shame
Then with a sort of air and grace
Took home the woman to her place:
A sergeant's widow, whom we knew
A decent sort of woman too.
Returned, his narrative he told
With illustrations manifold –
We thought indeed 'twas bravely done
But couldn't wholly lose our fun
And mocked and jested at it still
The more so that he took it ill.
     Ah, but we caught it by and bye!
By Jove, but didn't he let fly.
Young men, he said, were in their ways
Three times as bad as in old days.
We had such cold and careful ways
And hid our sins, and didn't dare
Our minds upon our brows to wear.
You cannot think how he went on:
All generosity was gone
High tone and spirit there was none
Thanked heaven he hadn't got a son.
Chivalry was forgotten quite;
No wonder that we couldn't fight

If Englishmen were of our make
Sebastopol we ne'er should take[31]
To say so he was truly grieved
And should be more, but he believed
The men than we were better far
And so good fortune to the war.
    At last he bid us all good-bye
And hope we'd live and wouldn't die
And some fine day with heaven's good grace
We'd take the blackguard of a place.
Tomorrow, if things didn't fail
He hoped for Scutari to sail.[32]
    The morrow we were scarcely out
When came the rumour all about
Our ancient merry friend they said
Had been indeed and gone ahead.
'He with the woman whom you know
To Scutari to-day will go
By Jove, the oddest thing in life
He's gone and took her for his wife!'

The second officer, who kept the watch,
A young man, fair of feature, partly Scotch
And partly Irish in his voice and look,
His portion thus in our diversion took.

THE MATE'S STORY

I've often wondered how it is at times
Good people do what are as bad as crimes.
A common person would have been ashamed
To do what once a family far-famed

31 After a long siege Sebastopol was stormed in 1855.
32 Scutari, facing Istanbul, was the location of the military hospital superintended
    by Florence Nightingale.

For their religious ways was known to do.
Small harm befell, small thanks to them were due.
They from abroad, perhaps it cost them less,
Had brought a young French girl as governess,
A pretty youthful thing as e'er you saw;
She taught the children how to play and draw,
Of course, the language of her native land;
English she scarcely learnt to understand.
After a time they wanted her no more;
She must go home, – but how to send her o'er, –
Far in the south of France she lived, and they
In Ireland there – was more than they could say.
A monthly steamer, as they chanced to know,
From Liverpool went over to Bordeaux,
And would, they thought, exactly meet the case.
They wrote and got a friend to take a place;
And from her salary paid her money down.
A trading steamer from the seaport town
Near where they lived, across the Channel plied,[33]
And this, they said, a passage would provide.
      With pigs, and with the Irish reaping horde,
This pretty tender girl was put on board;
And a rough time of it, no doubt, had she,
Tossing about upon the Irish Sea.
Arrived at last and set ashore, she found
The steamer gone for which she had been bound.
The pious people, in their careless way
Had made some loose mistake about the day.
She stood; the passengers with whom she crossed
Went off, and she remained as one that's lost.
      Think of the hapless creature standing here
Alone beside her boxes on the pier.
Whither to turn, and where to try and go,
Knew not; nay, the language did not know.

33 St George's Channel, not the English Channel.

So young a girl, so pretty too, set down
Here, in the midst of a great seaport town,
What might have happened one may sadly guess,
Had not the captain, seeing her distress,
Made out the cause, and told her she could stay
On board the vessel till the following day.
Next day he said; the steamer to Bordeaux
Was gone, no doubt, next month the next would go.
For this her passage-money she had paid,
But some arrangement could, he thought, be made,
If only she could manage to afford
To wait a month and pay for bed and board.
She sadly shook her head – well, after all,
'Twas a bad town, and mischief might befall.
Would she go back? Indeed, 'twas but a shame,
To take her back to those from whom she came.
'There's one thing, Miss,' said he 'that you can do;
It's speaking somewhat sudden-like, it's true,
But if you'll marry me, I'll marry you.
May be you won't, but if you will you can.'
This captain was a young and decent man,
And I suppose she saw no better way;
Marry they did, and married live this day.
          The Artillery Captain said 'twas well
There was no further incident to tell.
He'd been afraid that ere the tale was o'er
'Twould prove the captain had a wife before.
The poor French girl was luckier than she knew;
Soldiers and sailors had so often two.
And it was something, too, for men who went
From port to port to be with two content.
In every place the marriage rite supplied
A decent spouse, to whom you were not tied.
Of course the women would at times suspect,
But felt their reputations were not wrecked.

Mari Magno

The Fifth Night

One after night we took ourselves to task
For our neglect, who had forborne to ask
The clergyman, who told his tale so well,
Another tale for our behalf to tell.
He to a second had himself confessed.
Now, when to hear it eagerly we pressed,
He put us off; but, ere the night was done,
Told us his second, and his sadder one.

THE CLERGYMAN'S SECOND TALE

Edward and Jane a married couple were,
And fonder she of him or he of her
Were hard to say; their wedlock had begun
When in one year they both were twenty-one,
And friends, who would not sanction, left them free.
He gentle born, nor his inferior she,
And neither rich; to the new-wedded boy
A great Insurance Office found employ.
Strong in their loves and hopes, with joy they took
This narrow lot, and the world's altered look;
Beyond their home they nothing sought or craved,
And even from the narrow income saved;
Their busy days for no ennui had place,
Neither grew weary of the other's face.
Nine happy years had crowned their married state
With children, one a little girl of eight;
With nine industrious years his income grew,
With his employers rose his favour too;
Nine years complete had passed when something ailed,
Friends and the doctors said his health had failed,
He must recruit, or worse would come to pass;
And though to rest was hard for him, alas!

Three months of leave he found he could obtain,
And go, they said, get well and work again.
       Just at this juncture of their married life,
Her mother, sickening, begged to have his wife.
Her house among the hills in Surrey stood,
And to be there, said Jane, would do the children good.
They let their house, and with the children she
Went to her mother, he beyond the sea;
Far to the south his orders were to go.
A watering-place, whose name we need not know,
For climate and for change of scene was best:
There he was bid, laborious task, to rest.
       A dismal thing in foreign lands to roam
To one accustomed to an English home,
Dismal yet more, in health if feeble grown,
To live a boarder, helpless and alone
In foreign town: and worse yet worse is made,
If 'tis a town of pleasure and parade.
Dispiriting the public walks and seats,
The alien faces that an alien meets,
Drearily every day this old routine repeats.[34]
Yet here this alien prospered, change of air
Or change of scene did more than tenderest care;
Three weeks were scarce completed, to his home,
He wrote to say, he thought he now could come,
His usual work was sure he could resume,
And something said about the place's gloom,
And how he loathed idling his time away.
O, but they wrote, his wife and all, to say
He must not think of it, 'twas quite too quick;
Let was their house, her mother still was sick,
Three months were given, and three he ought to take,
For his and hers and for his children's sake.

---

34 Here Clough's MS contains the lines: 'The caterers for amusement in the streets
   / Accosting still, whom he must still refuse'.

He wrote again, 'twas weariness to wait,
This doing nothing was a thing to hate;
He'd cast his nine laborious years away,
And was as fresh as on his wedding-day;
At last he yielded, feared he must obey.
        And now, his health repaired, his spirits grown
Less feeble, less he cared to live alone.
'Twas easier now to walk the crowded shore,
The table d'hôte less tedious than before;
His ancient silence sometimes he would break
And the mute Englishman was heard to speak.
His youthful colour soon, his youthful air
Came back; amongst the busy idlers there,
With whom good looks entitle to good name,
For his good looks he gained a sort of fame;
People would watch him as he went and came.
        Explain the tragic mystery who can,
Something there is, we know not what, in man,
With all established happiness at strife,
And bent on revolution in his life.
Explain the plan of Providence who dare,
And tell us wherefore in his world there are
Beings who seem for this alone to live,
Temptation to another soul to give.
A beauteous woman at the table d'hôte
To try this English heart, at least to note
This English countenance, conceived the whim.
She sat exactly opposite to him.
Ere long he noticed with a vague surprise
How every day she bent on him her eyes;
Soft and enquiring how they looked, and then
Wholly withdrawn, unnoticed came again;
His shrunk aside: and yet there came a day,
Alas! they did not wholly turn away[35]

35 Here Clough's MS contains the lines 'Turned, but like hers returned; and yet
    and yet / The days drew on, and conscious glances met'.

So beautiful her beauty was, so strange,
And to his northern feeling such a change;
Her throat and neck Junonian in their grace;
The blood just mantled in her southern face:
Dark hair, dark eyes; and all the arts she had
With which some dreadful power adorns the bad, –
Bad women in their youth; – and young was she, –
Twenty perhaps, at the utmost twenty-three,
And timid seemed, and innocent of ill; –
Her feelings went and came without her will.
Her youthful feelings overcame her still
Timid at first, a little thing might daunt
And a harsh look be taken as a taunt.
Changing anon – but simply I should fail
Should I attempt her changes to detail.
Nor will you wish minutely to know all
His efforts in the prospect of the fall.
He oscillated to and fro, he took
High courage oft, temptation from him shook,
Compelled himself to virtuous acts and just,
And as it were in ashes and in dust
Abhorred his thought. But living thus alone,
Of solitary tedium weary grown;
From sweet society so long debarred,
And fearful in his judgement to be hard
On her – that he was sometimes off his guard
What wonder? She relentless still pursued
Unmarked, and tracked him in his solitude.[36]
      Going to his room, one day, upon the stair
Above him he perceived her lingering there;
Upon the stair she lingered; at the top,
As though till he should follow, seemed to stop,
And when he followed, moved – and yet looked round

36 The 1869 edition alters some of the preceding lines to make the text consistent
with a subsequent omission.

And seeming as if waiting to be found
At her half-open chamber door she stood;
A sudden madness mounted in his blood
And took him in a moment to the place;
He stopped, and seeking swift the half-hidden face
There, with the exultation of a boy,
Read in her liquid eyes the passion of her joy;
And went in with her at the fatal door
When he reissued innocent no more.[37]

    Two days elapsed and found him in this flame
And left him: on the third a letter came
From home; indeed it had been long delayed,
The mother's illness had the occasion made;[38]
Came from his wife, the little daughter too
In a large hand – the exercise was new –
To her papa her love and kisses sent: –
Into his very heart and soul it went.
Forth on the high and dusty road he sought
Some issue for the vortex of his thought;
Returned, packed up his things, and ere the day
Descended, was a hundred miles away.

    There are, I know, of course, who lightly treat
Such slips; we stumble, we regain our feet;
What can we do, they say, but hasten on
And disregard it as a thing that's gone?
Many there are who in a case like this
Would calm re-seek their sweet domestic bliss
Accept unshamed the wifely tender kiss,
And lift their little children on their knees,
And take their kisses too; with hearts at ease
Will read the household prayers, – to church will go
And sacrament, – nor care if people know.

37 The preceding fourteen lines were omitted by Blanche Clough in 1869.
38 The 1869 edition alters these lines to adapt them to the previous omission.

Such men, – so minded – do exist, God knows,
And, God be thanked, this was not one of those.
          Late in the night at a provincial town
In France a passing traveller was put down;
Haggard he looked, his hair was turning grey,
His hair, his clothes, were much in disarray:
In a bedchamber here one day he stayed,
Wrote letters, posted them, his reckoning paid,
And went. 'Twas Edward four days from his fall;
Here to his wife he wrote and told her all.
Forgiveness – yes perhaps she might forgive:
For her, and for the children, he must live
At any rate; but their old home to share
As yet was something that he could not bear.
She with her mother still her home should make,
A lodging near the office he should take;
And once a quarter he would bring his pay,
And he would see her on the quarter-day.
But her alone; e'en this would dreadful be,
The children 'twas not possible to see.
          Back to the office at this early day
To see him come, old-looking thus and grey
His comrades wondered, wondered too to see
How dire a passion for his work had he,[39]
How in a garret too he lived alone;
So cold a husband, cold a father grown.
          In a green lane beside her mother's home,
Where in old days they had been used to roam,
His wife had met him on the appointed day,
Fell on his neck, said all that love could say,
And wept; he put the loving arms away.
At dusk they met, for so was his desire;

---

39 Here Clough's MS contains the lines 'And seldom spoke, and scarcely showed
    his face / And was the worst companion in the place'.

She felt his cheeks and forehead all on fire;
The kisses which she gave he could not brook;
Once in her face he gave a sidelong look,
Said, but for them he wished that he were dead,
And put the money in her hand and fled.
      Sometimes, in easy and familiar tone,
Of sins resembling more or less his own
He hears his comrades in the office speak,
And felt the colour tingling in his cheek;
Lightly they spoke as of a thing of nought;
He of their judgement ne'er so much as thought.
      I know not, in his solitary pains,
Whether he seemed to feel as in his veins
The moral mischief circulating still,
Writhed with the torture of a double will;
And like a frontier land where armies wage
The mighty wars, engage and yet engage
All through the summer in the fierce campaign;
March, counter-march, gain, lose, and yet regain;
With battle reeks the desolated plain;
So felt his nature yielded to the strife
Of the contending good and ill of life.
      But a whole year this penance he endured,
Nor even then would think that he was cured.
Once in the quarter, in the country lane,
He met his wife and paid his quarter's gain;
To bring the children she besought in vain.
      He has a life small happiness that gives,
Who friendless in a London lodging lives,
Dines in a dingy chop-house, and returns
To a lone room, while all within him yearns
For sympathy, and his whole nature burns
With a fierce thirst for some one, – is there none? –
To expend his human tenderness upon.
So blank and hard and stony is the way
To walk, I wonder not men go astray

Unhappy he who in such temper meets
(Sisters in pain) the unhappy of the streets.[40]
     Edward, whom still a sense that never slept
On the strict path undeviating kept,
One winter evening found himself pursued
Amidst the dusky thronging multitude,
By a poor flaunting creature of the town
In crumpled bonnet and in faded gown
With tarnished flowers and ribbons hanging down.[41]
Quickly he walked, but strangely swift was she,
And pertinacious, and would make him see.
He saw at last, and recognising slow,
Discovered in this hapless thing of woe
The occasion of his shame twelve wretched months ago.
She gaily laughed, she cried, and sought his hand,
And spoke sweet phrases of her native land;
Exiled, she said, her lovely home had left
Not to forsake a friend of all but her bereft;
Exiled, she cried, for liberty, for love,
She was; still limpid eyes she turned above.
So beauteous once, and now this misery in,
Pity had all but softened him to sin.
But while she talked and still in his despite
Called to his mind the dreadful past delight,
And wildly laughed and miserable cried
And plucked the hand, which sadly he denied,
A stranger came, and swept her from his side.
     He watched them in the gas-lit darkness go
And a voice said within him, Even so,
So midst the gloomy mansions where they dwell
The lost souls walk the flaming streets of hell!
The lamps appeared to fling a baleful glare,
A brazen heat was heavy in the air;

---

40 This and the preceding line were omitted by Blanche Clough in 1869.
41 This and the preceding two lines also were omitted.

And it was hell, and he some unblest wanderer there.
       For a long hour he staid the streets to roam,
Late, gathering sense, he gained his garret home;
There found a telegraph that bade him come
Straight to the country, where his daughter, still
His darling child, lay dangerously ill.
The doctor would he bring? Away he went,
And found the doctor; to the office sent
A letter, asking leave; and went again,
And with a wild confusion in his brain
Joining the doctor caught the latest train.
The train swift whirled them from the city light
Into the shadows of the natural night.
       'Twas silent starry midnight on the down,
Silent and chill, when, they, straight come from town,
Leaving the station, walked a mile to gain
The lonely house amid the hills where Jane,
Her mother, and her children could be found.
Waked by their entrance out of sleep unsound,
The child not yet her altered father knew;
Yet talked of her papa in her delirium too.
Danger there was, yet hope there was; and he,
To attend the crisis, and the changes see,
And take the steps, at hand should surely be.
       Said Jane, the following day, 'Edward, you know,
Over and over I have told you so,
As in a better world I seek to live,
As I desire forgiveness, I forgive;
Forgiveness does not feel the word to say.
As I believe in One who takes away
Our sin and gives us righteousness instead, –
You to this sin, I do believe, are dead.
'Twas I, you know, who let you leave your home
And bid you stay when you so wished to come;
My fault was that: I've told you so before,
And vainly told; but now it's something more.
Say, is it right, without a single friend,

Without advice, to leave me to attend
Children and mother both? Indeed I've thought
Through want of you the child her fever caught.
Chances of mischief come with every hour;
And 'tis not in a single woman's power
Alone, and ever haunted more or less
With anxious thoughts of you and your distress, –
'Tis not indeed, I'm sure of it, in me –
All things with perfect judgement to foresee.
This weight has grown too heavy to endure;
And you, I tell you now, and I am sure,
Neglect your duty both to God and man
Persisting thus in your unnatural plan.
This feeling you must conquer, for you can.
And, after all, you know we are but dust,
What are we, in ourselves, that we should trust?
            He scarcely answered her; but he obtained
A longer leave, and quietly remained.
Slowly the child recovered, long was ill,
Long delicate, and he must watch her still;
To give up seeing her he could not bear;
To leave her less attended, did not dare.
The child recovered slowly, slowly too
Recovered he, and more familiar drew
Home's happy breath. All apprehension o'er,
Their former life he yielded to restore,
And to his mournful garret went no more.

———————————

            Midnight was dim and hazy overhead
When the tale ended and we turned to bed.
On the companion-way, descending slow,
The Artillery Captain, as we went below,
Said to the lawyer, life could not be meant
To be so altogether innocent.

What did the atonement show? He, for the rest,
Could not, he thought, have written and confessed.
Weakness it was, and adding crime to crime
To leave his family that length of time,
The lawyer said. The American was sure
Each nature knows instinctively its cure.
　　　　Midnight was in the cabin still and dead,
Our fellow passengers were all in bed;
We followed them, and nothing further spoke.
Out of the sweetest of my sleep I woke
At two, and felt we stopped; amid a dream
Of England knew the letting off of steam
And rose. 'Twas fog, and were we off Cape Race?
The captain would be certain of his place.
Wild in white vapour flew away the force
And self-arrested was the eager course
That had not ceased before. But shortly now
Cape Race was made to starboard on the bow.
The paddles plied. I slept. The following night
In the mid seas we saw a quay and light,
And peered through mist into an unseen town,
And on scarce-seeming land set one companion down,
And went. With morning and a shining sun,
Under the bright New Brunswick coast we run,
And visible discern to every eye
Rocks, pines, and little ports, and passing by
The boats and coasting craft. When sunk the night,
Early now sunk, the northern streamers bright
Floated and flashed the cliffs and clouds behind,
With phosphorus the billows all were lined.
　　　　That evening, while the Arctic streamers bright
Rolled from the clouds in waves of airy light,
The lawyer said, 'I laid by for to-night
A story that I would not tell before:
For the last time, a confidential four
We meet. Receive in your elected ears
A tale of human suffering and tears.

167

Mari Magno

[*The Last Night*]

THE LAWYER'S SECOND TALE
Christian

A Highland inn among the Western hills,
A single parlour, single bed that fills
With fisher or with tourist, as may be;
A waiting-maid, as fair as you can see,
With hazel eyes, and frequent-blushing face,
And ample brow, and with a rustic grace
In all her easy quiet motions seen,
Large of her age, which haply is nineteen;
Christian her name, in full a pleasant name,
Christie and Chirstie scarcely seem the same; –
A college fellow, who has sent away
The pupils he has taught for many a day,
And comes for fishing and for solitude,
Perhaps a little pensive in his mood,
An aspiration and a thought have failed,
Where he had hoped, another has prevailed,
But to the joys of hill and stream alive,
And in his boyhood yet, at twenty-five.
　　　　A merry dance, that made young people meet,
And set them moving both with hands and feet;
A dance in which he danced, and nearer knew
The soft brown eyes, and found them tender too;
A dance that lit in two young hearts the fire,
The low soft flame, of loving sweet desire,
And made him feel that he could feel again; –
The preface this, what follows to explain.
　　　　That night he kissed, he held her in his arms
And felt the subtle virtue of her charms;
Nor less bewildered on the following day
He kissed, he found excuse near her to stay, –

Was it not love? And yet the truth to speak,
Playing the fool for haply half a week,
He yet had fled, so strong within him dwelt
The horror of the sin, and such he felt
The miseries to the woman that ensue.
  She, simple child, all this that little knew,
If e'er he frowned and words of trouble said,
Deemed that for means to meet he vexed his head.
  Katie, the other lassie, who was cook,
All of herself the crisis undertook;
Found him apart, and little speech to spare,
Yet whispered clear the how, the when, the where
E'en for to-night. She went: and out he reeled
Into the air, and paced about the field.
Horror and grief! There pacing to and fro
Perceived the one solution was to go.
Thrice to his room to pack his knapsack went,
Clothes at the wash, not ready, thrice prevent.
It seems till evening he must bear to stay;
So for the while upon a rugged way
He wandered out, and still his reasonings ran,
Prevision is the attribute of man,
The women from the women we must save,
And interpose to hold them from the grave.[42]
He wearied long his brain with reasonings fine,
But when at evening dusk he came to dine,
In linsey petticoat and jacket blue
She stood, so radiant and so modest too,
All into air his strong conclusions flew.
The things he wanted in his room he'd find,
She'd *wrought* all afternoon: – how good, how kind![43]
Now should he go. But dim and drizzling too,
For a night march to night will hardly do,

---

42 The preceding nineteen lines were omitted by Blanche Clough in 1869.
43 These two lines, with their backward reference, were likewise omitted.

A march of sixteen weary miles of way;
No, by the chances, which our lives obey
No, by the Heavens and this sweet face, he'll stay.
　　　In linsey petticoat and jacket blue
She looked so lovely and so modest too,
And, dinner done, so quietly withdrew.
Worn with the mental conflicts of the day
He sat and slept three solid hours away.
So with her thickest concave of still air
Deep night descends, and how, and when, and where
In council meet, and plying swift their charms
Convey the sweet companion to his arms; –
　　　Next morning, quick, that none shall see or say,
He to the streams will go and fish all day:
All day he fished: late coming from the hill
He dined, and sat, and letters wrote; until
Deep night again descended, dark and still,
And how, and when, and where their charms renewed,
And the fond lover with his love endued.
　　　A week these prudent loves endured; but then
She feared, and said he'd better go again:[44]
Her time of service shortly would be o'er,
And she would leave; her mistress knew before.
Where would she go? To Glasgow, if she could, –
Her father's sister would be kind and good;
An only child she was, an orphan left,
Of all her kindred, save of this, bereft.
Said he, 'Your guide to Glasgow let me be,
You little know, you have not tried the sea;
Say, at the ferry when are we to meet?
Thither, I guess, you travel on your feet.'
She would be there on Tuesday next at three;
O dear, how glad and thankful she would be;
'But don't,' she said, 'be troubled much for me.'

44　The preceding eighteen lines also were omitted.

Punctual they met, a second class he took
More naturally to her wants to look,
And from her side was seldom far away.
So quiet, so indifferent yet, were they,
As fellow-servants travelling south they seemed,
And no one of a love-relation dreamed.
At Oban, where the stormy darkness fell,
He got two chambers in a cheap hotel.
At Oban of discomfort one is sure,
Little the difference whether rich or poor.
Around the Mull the passage now to make
They go aboard, and separate tickets take,
First-class for him, and second-class for her.
No other first-class passengers there were,
And with the captain walking soon alone,
This Highland girl, he said, to him was known,
He had engaged to take her to her kin;
Could she be put the ladies' cabin in?
The difference gladly he himself would pay,
The weather seemed but menacing to-day.
She ne'er had travelled from her home before,
He wished to be at hand to hear about her more.
Curious it seemed, but he had such a tone,
And kept at first so carefully alone,
And she so quiet was and so discreet,
So heedful ne'er to seek him or to meet,
The first small wonder quickly passed away.
And so from Oban's little land-locked bay
Forth out to Jura – Jura pictured high
With lofty peaks against the western sky,
Jura, that far o'erlooks the Atlantic seas,
The loftiest of the Southern Hebrides.
Through the main sea to Jura; when we reach
Jura, we turn to leftward to the breach,
And southward strain the narrow channel through,
And Colonsay we pass and Islay too

Kintyre is on the left; and all the day
A dull dead calm upon the waters lay.
        Sitting below, after some length of while
He sought her, and the tedium to beguile
He ventured some experiments to make,
The measure of her intellect to take.
Upon the cabin table chanced to lie
A book of popular astronomy;
In this he tried her, and discoursed away
Of Winter, Summer, and of Night and Day.
Still to the task a reasoning power she brought
And followed, slowly followed with the thought;
How beautiful it was to see the stir
Of natural wonder waking thus in her;
But loth was he to set on books to pore
An intellect so charming in the ore.
        And she, perhaps, had comprehended soon
Even the nodes so puzzling of the moon;[45]
But nearing now the Mull they met the gale
Right in their teeth: and should the fuel fail?
Thinking of her, he grew a little pale,
But bravely she the terrors, miseries, took:
And met him with a sweet courageous look:
Once, at the worst, unto his side she drew,
And said a little tremulously too,
'If we must die, please let me come to you.'
        I know not by what change of wind or tide,
Heading the Mull, they gained the Eastern side,
But stiller now, and sunny e'en it grew,
Arran's high peaks unmantled to the view;
While to the North, far seen from left to right,
The Highland range extended snowy white.
        Now in the Clyde, he asked what would be thought

---

45 The nodes are the points at which the plane of the moon's orbit cuts the ecliptic,
i.e. the apparent trajectory of the sun.

In Glasgow of the company she brought
'You know,' he said 'how I desire to stay;
We've played at strangers for so long a day,
But for a while I yet would go away.'
     She said, O no, indeed they must not part.
Her father's sister had a kindly heart.
'I'll tell her all, and O, when you she sees,
I think she'll not be difficult to please.'
     Landed at Glasgow, quickly they espied
Macfarlane, grocer, by the river side:
To greet her niece the woman joyful ran,
But looked with wonder on the tall young man.
Into the house the women went and talked,
He with the grocer in the doorway walked.
He told him he was looking for a set
Of lodgings: had he any he could let?
     The man was called to council with his wife;
They took the thing as what will be in life,
Half in a kind, half in a worldly way;
They said, the lassie might play out her play.
The gentleman should have the second floor,
At thirty shillings, for a week or more.
     Some days in this obscurity he stayed,
Happy with her, and some inquiry made
(For friends he found) and did his best to see
What hope of getting pupils there would be.
This must he do, 'twas evident, 'twas clear,
Marry and seek a humble maintenance here.
Himself he had a hundred pounds a year.
To this plain business he would bend his life,
And find his joy in children and in wife,
A wife so good, so tender, and so true,
Mother to be of glorious children too.
     Half to excuse his present lawless way,
He to the grocer happened once to say
Marriage would cost him more than others dear,

173

Cost him, indeed, three hundred pounds a year.
''Deed' said the man, 'a heavy price no doubt,
For a bit form that one can do without.'
And asked some questions, pertinent and plain,
Exacter information to obtain;
He took a little trouble to explain.

      The College Audit now, to last at least
Three weeks, ere ending with the College Feast,[46]
He must attend, a tedious, dull affair,
But he, as Junior Bursar, must be there.
Three weeks, however, quickly would be fled,
And then he'd come – he didn't say to wed.

      With plans of which he nothing yet would say
Preoccupied, upon the parting day
He seemed a little absent and distrait;
But she, as knowing nothing was amiss,
Gave him her fondest smile, her sweetest kiss.

      A fortnight after, or a little more,
As at the Audit, weary of the bore,
He sat, and of his future prospects thought,
A letter in an unknown hand was brought.
'Twas from Macfarlane, and to let him know
To South Australia they proposed to go.
'Rich friends we have, who have advised us thus,
Occasion offers suitable for us;
Chirstie we take; whate'er she find of new
She'll ne'er forget the joys she's had with you;
'Tis an expensive pilgrimage to make,
You'll like to send a trifle for her sake.'
Nothing he said of when the ship would sail.

      That very night, by swift returning mail,
Ten pounds he sent, for what he did not know;

---

46 At the annual audit the College accounts for the year were made up, super-
vised by two fellows nominated as Bursars, and a dividend was distributed to
the fellows.

And 'In no case' he said 'let Christian go.'
He in three days would come, and for his life
Would claim her and declare her as his wife.
        Swift the night mail conveyed his missive on;
He followed in three days, and found them gone.
All three had sailed: he looked as if he dreamed;
The money-order had been cashed, it seemed.

        The Clergyman, 'This story is mere pain,'
Exclaimed, 'for if the women don't sustain
The moral standard, all we do is vain.'
        'But what we want,' the Yankee said, 'to know
Is if the girl went willingly or no.
Sufficient motive though one does not see,
'Tis clear the grocer used some trickery.'

        He judged himself, so strong the clinging in
This kind of people is to kith and kin;
For if they went and she remained behind,
No one she had, if him she failed to find.
Alas, this lawless loving was the cause,
She did not dare to think how dear she was.
Justly his guilty tardiness was curst,
He should have owned her when he left her first.
And something added how upon the sea,
She perilled, too, a life that was to be;
A child that, born in far Australia, there
Would have no father and no father's care.
So to the South a lonely man returned,
For other scenes and busier life he burned, –
College he left and settled soon in town,
Wrote in the journals, gained a swift renown.
Soon into high society he came,
And still where'er he went outdid his fame.
All the more liked and more esteemed, the less
He seemed to make an object of success.

175

Mari Magno

An active literary life he spent,
Toward lofty points of public practice bent,
Was never man so carefully who read,
Whose plans so well were fashioned in his head
Nor one who truths so luminously said.
Some years in various labours thus he passed,
A spotless course maintaining to the last.
Twice upon Government Commissions served
With honour; place, which he declined, deserved.
He married then, – a marriage fit and good,
That kept him where his worth was understood;
A widow, wealthy and of noble blood.
Mr and Lady Mary are they styled;
One grief is theirs – to be without a child.
    I did not tell you how he went before
To South Australia, vainly to explore.
The ship had come to Adelaide, no doubt;
Watching the papers he had made it out,
But of themselves, in country or in town,
Nothing discovered, travelling up and down.
Only an entry, of uncertain sound,
In an imperfect register he found.
His son, he thought, but could not prove it true;
The surname of the girl it chanced he never knew.
    But this uneasy feeling gathered strength
As years advanced, and it became at length
His secret torture and his secret joy
To think about his lost Australian boy.
Somewhere in wild colonial lands has grown
A child that is his true and very own.
This strong parental passion fills his mind,
To all the dubious chances makes him blind.
Still he will seek, and still he hopes to find.
Yet will he go.

            Said I, 'O let him stay

And in a London drawing room some day –
Rings on her fingers, brilliants in her hair,
The lady of the latest millionaire –
She'll come, and with a gathering slow surprise
On Lady Mary's husband turn the eyes,
The soft brown eyes that in a former day
From his discretion lured him all astray.
At home, six bouncing girls, who more or less
Are learning English of a governess,
Six boisterous boys, as like as pear to pear;
Only the eldest has a different air.'

      'You jest,' he said, 'indeed it happened so.'
From a great party just about to go
He saw, he knew, and ere she saw him, said
Swift to his wife, and for the doorway made,
'My Highland bride! To escape a scene I go,
Stay, find her out – great God! – and let me know.'
      The Lady Mary turned to scrutinise
The lovely brow, the beautiful brown eyes,
One moment, then performed her perfect part,
And did her spiriting with simplest art;
Was introduced, her former friends had known;
Say, might she call to-morrow afternoon
At three? O yes! At three she made her call,
And told her who she was and told her all.
Her lady manners all she laid aside;
Like women the two women kissed and cried.
Half overwhelmed sat Christian by her side,
While she, 'You know he never knew the day
When you would sail, but he believed you'd stay
Because he wrote – you never knew, you say, –
Wrote that in three days' time, they need not fear,
He'd come and then would marry you, my dear.
You never knew? And he had planned to live
At Glasgow, lessons had arranged to give.

177

Alas, then to Australia he went out,
All through the land to find you sought about,
And found a trace which, though it left a doubt,
Sufficed to make it still his grief, his joy,
To think he had a child, a living boy,
Whom you, my love – '
                'His child is six foot high,
I've kept him as the apple of my eye,'
Cried she, 'he's riding, or you'd see him here.
O joy, that he at last should see his father dear!
As soon as he comes in I'll tell him all,
And on his father he shall go and call.'
        'And you,' she said, 'my husband will you see?'
        'O no, it is not possible for me.
The boy I'll send this very afternoon.
O dear, I know he cannot go too soon;
And something I must write, to write will do.'
So they embraced and sadly bade adieu.
        The boy came in, his father went and saw, –
We will not wait this interview to draw –
Ere long returned, and to his mother ran:
His father was a wonderful fine man,
He said and looked at her; the Lady, too,
Had done whatever it was kind to do.
He loved his mother more than he could say,
But if she wished, he'd with his father stay.
A little change she noticed in his face,
E'en now the father's influence she could trace.
From her the slight, slight severance had begun,
But simply she rejoiced that it was done.
She smiled and kissed her boy, and 'Long ago,
When I was young, I loved your father so.
Together now we had been living, too,
Only the ship went sooner than he knew.
In loving him you will be loving me:
Father and Mother are as one, you see.'

Her letter caught him on the following day
As to the club he started on his way.
From her he guessed, the hand indeed was new;
Back to his room he went and read it through
          'I know not how to write, and dare not see;
But it will take a load of grief from me –
O! what a load – that you at last should know
The way in which I was compelled to go.
Wretched, I know, and yet it seems 'twas more
Cruel and wretched than I knew before;
So many years to think how on your day
Joyful you'd come, and find me flown away.
What would you think of me, what would you say?
O love, this little let me call you so;
What other name to use I do not know.
O let me think that by your side I sit,
And tell it you, and weep a little bit,
And you too weep with me for hearing it.
Alone so long I've borne this dreadful weight:
Such grief, at times it almost turned to hate.
O let me think you sit, and listening long,
Comfort me still, and say I wasn't wrong,
And pity me, and far, far hence again
Dismiss, if haply any yet remain,
Hard thoughts of me that in your heart have lain.
O love! To hear your voice I dare not go;
But let me trust that you will judge me so.
          'I think no sooner were you gone away,
My aunt began to tell me of some pay
More than three hundred pounds a year 'twould be,
Which you, she said, would lose by marrying me.
Was this a thing a man of sense would do?
Was I a fool, to look for it from you?
You were a handsome gentleman and kind,
And to do right were every way inclined,
But to this truth I must submit my mind,

179

You would not marry. "Speak, and tell me true,
Say, has he ever said one word to you
That meant as much?" O, love, I knew you would,
I'd read it in your eyes so kind and good.
Although you did not speak, I understood.
Though for myself, indeed, I sought it not,
It seemed so high, so undeserved a lot,
But for the child, when it should come, I knew –
O, I was certain – what you meant to do.
        'Said she "We quit the land, will it be right
Or kind to leave you for a single night,
Just on the chance that he will come down here,
And sacrifice three hundred pounds a year,
And all his hopes and prospects fling away,
And has already had his will, as one may say?
Go you with us, and find beyond the seas
Men by the score to choose from, if you please."
        'I said my will and duty was to stay,
Wouldn't they help me to some decent way
To wait, and surely near was now the day?
Quite they refused. Had they to let you know
Written, I asked, to say we were to go?
They told me yes; they showed a letter too,
Post-office order that had come from you.
Alas, I could not read or write, they knew.
I think they meant me, though they did not say,
To think you wanted me to go away.
O, love, I'm thankful nothing of the kind
Ever so much as came into my mind.
        'To-morrow was the day that would not fail;
For Adelaide the vessel was to sail.
All night I hoped some dreadful wind would rise,
And lift the seas and rend the very skies.
All night I lay and listened still for you.
Twice to the door I went, the bolt I drew,
And called to you; scarce what I did I knew.

'Morning grew light, the house was emptied clear,
The ship would go, the boat was lying near.
They had my money, how was I to stay?
Who could I go to, when they went away?
Out in the streets I could not lie, you know.
O dear, but it was terrible to go.
Yet, yet I looked; I do not know what passed,
I think they took and carried me at last.
Twelve hours I lay, I sobbed in my distress;
But in the night "Let be this idleness,"
I said, "I'll bear it for my baby's sake,
Lest of my going mischief it should take;
Advice will seek, and every caution use;
My love I've lost – his child I must not lose."
     'How oft I thought, when sailing on the seas,
Of our dear journey through the Hebrides,
When you the kindest were and best of men:
O, love, I did not love you right till then.
O, and myself how willingly I blamed,
So simple who had been, and was ashamed,
And mindful only of the present joy,
When you had anxious care your busy mind to employ.
Ah well, I said, but now at least he's free,
He will not have to lower himself for me.
He will not lose three hundred pounds a year,
In many ways my love has cost him dear.
     'Upon the passage, great was my delight
A lady taught me how to read and write.
She saw me much, and fond of me she grew,
Only I durst not talk to her of you.
     'We had a quiet time upon the seas
And reached our port of Adelaide with ease.
At Adelaide my lovely baby came.
Philip, he took his father's Christian name,
And my poor maiden surname, to my shame.
O, but I little cared, I loved him so,

'Twas such a joy to watch and see him grow.
At Adelaide we made no length of stay;
Our friends to Melbourne just had gone their way.
We followed shortly where they led before,
To Melbourne went, and flourished more and more.
My aunt and uncle both are buried there;
I closed their eyes, and I was left their heir.
They meant me well, I loved them for their care.
    'Ten years ago I married Robert; dear
And well he loved and waited many a year.
Selfish it seemed to turn from one so true,
And I of course was desperate of you.
I've borne him children six; we've left behind
Three little ones, whom soon I hope to find.
To my dear boy he ever has been kind.
    'Next week we sail, and I should be so glad,
Only to leave my boy will made me sad.
But yours he is by right – the grief I'll bear,
And at his age more easy he can spare,
Perhaps, a mother's than a father's care.
Indeed I think him like his father too;
He may be happier, probably, with you.
'Tis best, I know, nor will he quite forget
Some day will come perhaps and see his mother yet.
    'O heaven! Farewell – perhaps I've been to blame
To write as if it all were still the same.
Farewell, write not. – I will not seek to know
Whether you ever think of me or no.'
    O love, love, love, too late! The tears fell down.
He dried them up – and slowly walked to town.

    To bed with busy thoughts; the following day
Bore us expectant into Boston bay;

Mari Magno

With dome and steeple on the yellow skies
Upon the left we watched with curious eyes
The Puritan great Mother City rise.
Among the islets, winding in and round,
The great ship moved to her appointed ground.
We bade adieu, shook hands and went ashore
I and my friend have seen our friends no more.

ACTAEON

Over a mountain-slope with lentisk, and with abounding
Arbutus, and the red oak overtufted, 'mid a noontide
Now glowing fervidly, the Leto-born, the divine one,
Artemis, Arcadian wood-rover, alone, hunt-weary,
Unto a dell cent'ring many streamlets her foot unerring
Shaded a waterfall, where pellucid yet abundant
Streams from perpetual full-flowing sources a current:
Lower on either bank in sunshine flowered the oleanders:
Plenteous under a rock green herbage here to the margin
Grew with white poplars o'er crowning. She, thither arrived,
Unloosing joyfully the vest unfolded upon her,
Swift the divine shoulders discovering, swiftly revealing
Her maidenly bosom and all her beauty beneath it,
To the river waters overflowing to receive her
Yielded her ambrosial nakedness. But with an instant
Conscious, with the instant the immortal terrific anger
Flew to the guilty doer: that moment, where amid amply
Concealing plane leaves he the opportunity, pursued
Long fruitlessly, possessed, unwise, Actaeon, of hunters,
Hapless of Arcadian and most misguided of hunters,
Knew the divine mandate, knew fate directed upon him.
He, crouching furtively, with audacious tremulous glance,
Espied approaching, saw descending, disarraying,
And the unclad shoulders awestruck, awestruck let his eyes see
The maidenly bosom but not – dim fear fell upon them –
Not more had witnessed. Not, therefore, less the forest through
Ranging, their master ceasing thenceforth to remember,
With the instant together trooping came as to devour him

184

Actaeon

His dogs from the ambush. – Transformed suddenly before them,
He fled, an antlered stag wild with terror to the mountain.
She, the liquid stream in, her limbs carelessly reclining,
The flowing waters collected grateful about her.